Don't Tell My Mum

The Continuing Memories of a Confused Seventies Childhood

By

Alex Cotton

In Memory of my Dad

and his Amazing Technicolour House

INTRODUCTION

A lot of people seemed to find my first book 'Don't Look at Me in That Tone of Voice' amusing and most of them wanted to find out what happened next. I seem to be blessed with a very good memory for my early life (not always a good thing) so I delved back into my store of memories and started again. I hope you won't be disappointed but if you are, remember, you asked for it.

This book picks up more or less from where the last one left off., and starts from the last day at junior school. It's now 1973, I am twelve years old and about to start High School (and dreading it). I am still living in the bosom of my strange family and escaping to my Aunty Dolly's at every opportunity. My mother is still giving her nightly concerts to the neighbours via the kitchen window with Joan next door, they seem to be harmonizing a lot better now, I must say. My brother is four years old now and getting ready to start school himself. My dad is still doing his best to go unnoticed in the world while inwardly rewriting his own life to suit him better and I am still not convinced that I wasn't adopted.

So off we go again, hold tight and welcome to my teenage years.

CHAPTER ONE

Three Wheeled Cars and Training Bras

It was the last day of term in late July 1973 and because it was the last day we were allowed to go into school without wearing our uniforms. I don't mean we went in our underwear, we were allowed to go in our 'own' clothes. A couple of years earlier this would have been my worst nightmare, given that the clothes my mother used to make me wear would have sent a scarecrow puce with embarrassment. One of the happiest days of my life was the day I was given a school uniform, at last I could look the same as the other kids.

For the last two years or so my mother had stopped knitting so much and had started letting let me wear clothes that the other kids were wearing - mostly. She could still surprise me now and then with some creation that she had spotted at a jumble sale or begged off some relative with bad eyesight and/or poor taste. Anyway, on this morning I waited for Melanie from next door to call for me and together we set off for what was to be our last day ever at junior school.

We didn't have to do any lessons on the last day so the teachers more or less left us to our own devices. I think they were just as relieved as we were that it was the end of our time there. For most of the day we just hung around talking and saying our goodbyes as some of us were going to different schools. One of the kids had brought in a record player, a little portable thing that looked like a suitcase and the teacher let us play records all day. It got a bit boring though as the girl who brought it only had three records, which meant six songs if you played the B sides and the B sides were usually rubbish.

In the afternoon, we had a big assembly in the hall so that the headmaster could wish us all well and send us on our way with a warning to keep out of trouble during the six
weeks summer holidays. Like anyone took any notice of that.

At the end of the day we had to go around to various classes to collect any projects that we had been working on during the year. We were encouraged to take our rubbish home so that our parents could put it in their own bins instead of the schools.

For some pupils, this meant they had to collect paintings, embroidered placemats or ceramic ashtrays. I had to collect my bedside cabinet. This was my woodwork project that I had been working on with the help of Mr Scott, the woodwork teacher. He was only five feet two and had such a bad limp that we all used to joke that he had a wooden leg that he had built himself. My bedside cabinet had started life as a jewellery box but I had confused the measurements and as a result cut the pieces of wood ten times bigger than they should have been. Mr Scott said it was too late to change it as I would be wasting too much wood and so my cabinet was born.

When my friend Michelle saw my cabinet in progress she was inspired to create a piece of bedroom furniture of her own. Much to Mr Scott's alarm, she decided she needed a wardrobe and after much arguing and haggling over the cost of the wood he let her have her own way. Our projects turned out wonderfully. In fact, my cabinet was so sturdy that twenty years later it was still going strong and ended up in my dad's greenhouse where he stored plant pots and bits and bobs in it.

When the leaving bell rang that afternoon we said our final goodbyes and headed off home for the summer holidays. I picked up my cabinet and struggled off home with it, I put my bags inside it so it made it a bit heavier but I managed. However, as long as I live I will never forget the sight of Michelle, staggering up the road with her wardrobe on her back.

She had opened the door so that she could get it onto her back easier and it looked as if she was wearing it. The only part of her that remained visible was her little legs sticking out of the bottom. Once she got going she was carried along by the momentum.

Luckily, she didn't have far to go and it was only a single wardrobe. I wonder if it lasted twenty years like my bedside cabinet.

That summer was a good one, I mentioned in the last book about getting my first boyfriend, even though we never actually spoke or looked at one another. After two weeks of nonexistent romance I had called the whole thing off leaving him none the wiser as I don't think he was aware that we were going out anyway. I decided I would be staying single for a while, though I don't think that would have been too difficult looking in the mirror. Let's just say that although there had been a big improvement in the last two years I was still going through my 'ugly duckling' phase.

A few months before, my mother had burst into my bedroom while I was practicing my dancing in my vest and knickers. She took one look and in a horrified tone told me to stop jiggling in my vest. Then she pointed at my chest and demanded to know when 'that' had happened. I didn't know what she meant at first until I realised she was pointing to the two small conkers that had appeared on my chest a few weeks earlier. I didn't know why she was making a fuss, I was hardly Dolly Parton.

Nevertheless, she told me to get dressed, we were going to buy me a bra. I was horrified as, going by past experience shopping with my mother I knew I was likely to end up with something hideous. I was worried she would buy me something like the thing she wore. The thing in question was an 'all in one' which consisted of a huge bra and girdle in one piece. It took her an eternity to put it on, there would be much huffing and puffing interspaced with the odd swear word and half a can of talcum powder. Because these contraptions were made of rubber she said the talc helped it to slip on easier. When she took it off again at night with more heaving and grunting she would release a cloud of talcum powder that would have us all choking. How the hell would I manage at school with one of these, what would I do when it was time for P.E or if I needed a wee? Now I had something else to worry about when I thought about starting High school.

Luckily, my fears proved ungrounded. She said I wouldn't need anything like that until I got bigger, how much bigger she didn't say. Anyway, a couple of hours later we were in the bra shop and the lady on the counter was shoving an assortment of bras at me in different patterns and colours. All the boxes said that they contained 'training' bras. I asked my mother what this meant and she replied that they trained your bosom. To do what, run a marathon? That woman never explained anything properly. Desperate to get out of the shop I picked the nearest one to me and tried to head for the door. No such luck, my mother said I had to try it on and shoved me into the changing room. I had never put on a bra before but I had seen my uncle in Derbyshire putting a bridle on a horse and it seemed to me to be very similar. The woman from the shop kept shouting through the curtain to ask if I needed help. I would scream back "No thank you", the last thing I needed was someone trying to help.

At last, the thing was on, I put my clothes back on and me and my bosom in training headed home. It felt horrible and uncomfortable, halfway home I realised it was also very itchy. Eventually my mother noticed me shimmying around and told me to stop twitching or people would think I was diabetic. I think she meant epileptic, there was no political correctness in those days.

That night, as we sat around the table for our tea my dad asked his usual question, "What have you been doing today."

"I got a bra". I announced.

This seemed to render him speechless, he turned bright red and became very engrossed in his chips. After that he didn't make eye contact with me for a week. He never handled the growing up thing very well, bless him.

Melanie was very jealous when she found out about my bra. She had been watching and waiting for ages for something to happen underneath her vest but sadly she remained flat as a pancake. I told her I would swap in an instant, I felt as if I was wearing a straight jacket (not that I had ever tried one).

Whenever one of us girls at school started to wear a bra, it provided the boys in the class with at least a week's worth of entertainment. They would take any and every opportunity to twang our bra straps and try to embarrass us. Some of the more adventurous ones would sit behind you and try to undo the clasp with a pencil, there was no such thing as sexual harassment back then.

For two girls our age who were discussing bras and waiting for our periods to start, me and Melanie were still as clueless as each other about everything else. Compared to today's twelve-year-old girls we were simpletons. A few weeks before the bra episode I had been listening to my mother and Joan from next door gossiping. They were looking at shoes in a catalogue, picking out something for Joan to wear to an upcoming wedding. I heard my mother saying that one pair would be nice if it wasn't for the ankle straps.

She said everybody knew the only women who wore ankle strap shoes were prostitutes. Straight away I asked what a prostitute was.

"Never you mind" came the reply.

It was my mother's stock answer whenever she didn't want to tell me anything.

Later that day I asked Melanie if she had ever heard of a prostitute. She thought for a minute then she said she thought it was like the reserve in netball. I pointed out that this was a substitute, not a prostitute so she had another think. She was sure she had heard the word before. After a few minutes, she remembered, she had seen it on the news. If you lived in Ireland, you were either a Catholic or a Prostitute and both sides hated each other.

This didn't make things any clearer. Did that mean that half the female population of Northern Ireland had to wear ankle strap shoes to prove that they weren't Catholic? It was all very confusing.

Anyway, back to the summer. I had decided to put the thought of 'big school' out of my head, I would deal with that when I had to. So, following my parent's example I buried it deep in the back of my brain and convinced myself that it wasn't happening.

That summer we went on a few day trips with my Aunty Dolly and her family. My Uncle Malcom had recently bought a Robin Reliant three wheeled car. It was similar to the one owned by Melanie's dad but his was a van, my Uncle Malcom's had a back seat and rear windows. Somehow, we all piled in it together, me, my brother and my parents were in the back with my cousin Malcom Junior. My Aunty Dolly and Uncle Malcom were in the front with my cousin Janice on Aunty Dolly's knee. Janice was sixteen now and nearly the same size as Aunty Dolly so that looked quite amusing.

We would never get away with it nowadays, it was like one of those things on the telly where they see how many people they can fit into a little car to break a record.

It was extremely uncomfortable to say the least but luckily, we got the chance to stretch our legs every time we came to a hill. There was no way the little car could make it up hills with all of us in it so everyone except Aunty Dolly and Uncle Malcom got out at the bottom of every hill. They would drive to the top and wait while the rest of us walked up the hill to meet them. At the top of the hill we would all climb back in and hurtle down the other side, it took quite a while to get to our destination. Usually we would stop for a picnic somewhere along the route, filling our faces with lemonade and sandwiches. Later on, everyone would moan at me for having to stop every twenty minutes to throw up. I still got car sick and no amount of travel sickness tablets could stop it. It didn't help to be squashed in the back of a miniature car with Malcom's armpits, my dad's sweaty feet and my mother's perfume which cost about 10p from the local market and could stop flies at fifty paces.

Sometimes we would go to the seaside, Withernsea or Bridlington. We'd walk round the shops eating ice creams (I would see mine again on the way home) and laughing at the rude postcards when my mother wasn't looking. My dad and Uncle Malcom would disappear to the nearest pub for a few pints (drinking and driving never seemed to worry anyone) while my Aunty Dolly would find the nearest bingo arcade and stay there until Uncle Malcom came back from the pub and forcibly removed her. Aunty Dolly had a serious bingo addiction and could smell out a game wherever we went.

We would go home with our pockets stuffed with sticks of rock and bags of mint humbugs. On the way, home my mother would treat us all to her rendition of 'I do like to be beside the seaside' while the rest of us prayed for a hill so we could get out for a break. It was great fun even if we, in the back couldn't walk properly again for a few days afterwards.

Some of the other days Melanie's parents would take us a bit nearer up the coast to play on the beach. Once again, it meant being squashed up in the back of a three- wheeled car among the deck chairs and picnic tables, although there was slightly more room as my brother and my parents stayed at home. Sometimes I marvel at the fact I can still stand upright considering all the time I spent crammed into the rear of extra small cars. It could explain why today I suffer from claustrophobia though.

CHAPTER TWO

Drag Queens and Luncheon Meat

That summer wasn't a good one for my dad. His factory was called out on strike and he was off work for weeks with no wages, just minimum strike pay. This was hardly enough to pay the rent, let alone pay for food and bills. My Aunty Dolly offered to help out but my dad was too proud, he wouldn't borrow or take handouts from anyone. My mother, on the other hand wasn't so proud and took what she could when my dad wasn't around. My dad said I couldn't visit Aunty Dolly's at mealtimes because it would look like I'd only gone for my dinner. This came as quite a blow to me; how would I get my sponge and custard fix now?

Luckily, Aunty Dolly was a step in front. She would do an extra bit for me and warm it up at whatever time I arrived. When I left to go home she would fill my pockets with biscuits (usually Penguins and Blue Ribands) and shove a couple of Custard Creams in my mouth for good measure. I would never go hungry while I had my Aunty Dolly.

Back at home, my mother wasn't coping well with having no money. Instead of doing the usual weekly shop at the supermarket she was confined to trying to find the cheapest things she could to feed us. Beans were on the menu every day but that was usual in our house, we ate them every day. They were cheap but it was mostly because, even at four years old they were still pretty much the only thing that my brother would eat. My mother still put a dollop of lard into the pan with them as she always had and always would for the next forty years or so. We never did find out why.

One of the cheapest things she found was Luncheon meat. My dad said it was made up of all the bits of other meats that were swept up at the end of the day. I don't think he meant off the floor but that's the picture that always popped into my head. A little man with a massive brush and shovel, picking through the rubbish for bits of meat. It tasted a bit like that as well.

Other mothers might have got a bit more inventive with the luncheon meat than mine. Some might have grilled it or made fritters with it, anything to make it seem like we weren't eating the same thing day in day out, not mine. She served it up for breakfast, dinner and tea, just sitting there on the plate, round and pink and limp and cold. She served it with chips and beans, mashed potatoes and beans, new potatoes and beans, just with beans. Sometimes, when we could take no more she would surprise us and serve peas. But then my brother wouldn't eat it.

I had the job, most days of running to the shop up the road to buy the never-ending supply of luncheon meat. To buy it, I had to go to the meat counter at the bottom of the shop, this counter was run by Ray. He was the campest man you ever saw. He had a bouffant that would have put Dusty Springfield in the shade and more jewellery than I had ever seen. Every time his hands flew across the meat slicer you would be dazzled by the shop lights reflecting off his gold plate and diamantes. I didn't know what 'camp' meant, I had never heard the word before but looking back now I can honestly say that Ray was camper than a row of pink tents at a camping convention.

He was always cheerful and loud and he would laugh and joke with all the women, usually about things to do with sausages and black pudding (I never got these jokes but all the women seemed to find them hilarious). I think he sensed when someone was a bit short of money because the less money you had, the thinner he would slice the meat. Our luncheon meat was practically transparent, we could see the pattern on our plates through it. Every day I would turn up at Ray's counter and stand, fascinated watching him do his bit. It was like he was putting on a show for the customers, sometimes he would even sing. Thank god, my mother didn't go in the shop much, she would have hopped up on the bacon slicer to accompany him.

A few years later I was flicking through the local paper and I came across an article about the latest act that had been booked to entertain people on the cross channel ferry. There was a photo to accompany the article. I couldn't believe my eyes, there, in all his glory and a big sequinned evening dress was Ray. In the billing, he was introduced as Ray/Julie Jackson, the most amazing drag queen ever. Things started to fall into place then. No wonder he had such bouncy hair and better legs than my mother, and I always wondered about the aroma of nail varnish that you could sometimes smell on our luncheon meat. I'm glad he eventually found his calling. I hope he's still out there on the ferries, sailing back and forth and continuing to get laughs about his giant chipolata.

My dad was bored to tears for all the weeks that he was on strike. He had never been out of work in his life and he didn't know what to do with himself. Every week he would go off to the meeting at his work in the hope that the strike would be called off and he could go back to work. It would be a couple of months before he got his wish so to pass the time he tried to keep himself occupied doing jobs around the house.

He went around touching up all the paintwork in all its wonderful colours, we still had the orange and yellow chessboard kitchen at this point. He found every loose screw in the house that he could and tightened them all up. He weeded the garden to within an inch of its life and cut the grass so often it was practically bald. When he ran out of jobs to do he decided to clear out every cupboard and drawer in the house. He always had a thing about cupboards and drawers being neat, tidy and free from clutter, I think it stemmed from his time in the army. For those few weeks, he drove my mother nuts, she couldn't find anything as he'd rearranged everything and thrown loads of things away. Every other day found my mother, head first in the dustbin trying to retrieve something that he thought she didn't need anymore.

After a few weeks of this my mother lost it and locked him out of the house, she wouldn't let him back in until he promised to leave her drawers alone. While he was out there he started on the shed. He had brought a label maker home from work and so he decided to label everything in there, and I mean everything. He labelled all his tools (although I thought you could easily recognise a hammer without a label), he labelled every box, carton and biscuit tin. He even labelled his boxes of gardening magazines, he was unstoppable. He labelled every drawer on the old cabinets that were in there, each label spelling out exactly what was in each drawer. Then when you opened the drawer he had labelled everything that was in there as well. If my mother hadn't stopped him I'm sure he would have made a label for the label maker.

One of his other shed obsessions were locks. He had a morbid fear of his shed being burgled so it had more security than Fort Knox. The shed door was locked with a key, then fitted with an extra yale lock and key. As well as this he fitted two padlocks top and bottom and to top it all he had an alarm that would go off if the door was opened. If Harry Houdini ever stopped by and managed to get through the door undetected he would have faced a lot more challenges inside. Each separate drawer had its own lock and also every cupboard door. Inside, any box or tin that he could fit a padlock on was also locked. Things like garden rakes, hoes and spades were wrapped tightly in metal chains that were padlocked and then the whole bundle was padlocked to a metal ring in the wall. His lawnmower was also chained and padlocked in the same way, it was amazing. If anyone had ever managed to get in during the night, it would have been mid-morning before they got half way through breaking all the locks.

Eventually, he ran out of things to do. Everything inside and out was painted, tidied, locked, sorted out and labelled. Luckily for him (and the rest of us) the strike was called off and he went back to work the week before I started high school. At last we could stop eating luncheon meat. I have never been able to face the stuff since but only a few weeks ago, my mother asked me to bring her some from the shops. She said she hadn't tasted any for ages and she just fancied some. Even more proof, if any were needed that she has finally lost her last marble.

Whenever I picture us all sitting around the table in those days I remember Twink. Twink was the tame sparrow that lived next door at Melanie's. Her dad had found him injured as a baby and nursed him back to health. When he was better he wouldn't leave so he lived in a budgie cage in the back garden. The cage door was left open all day so he could come and go as he pleased. He always knew when we were eating and he would fly through our back door and perch on my shoulder for a bit of my tea.

I thought this was great but my brother was terrified of Twink, he would have a hissy fit every time he flew in. Beans (with lard) would go flying as he scrambled frantically around trying to get away from the table. My dad would shout at him.

"Sit down you daft bugger, it's only a bird."

Meanwhile my brother would be screaming like a demented parrot and knocking things all over the place. My mother would be trying to defend him while trying not to scream herself as she had a phobia of flapping wings. It livened meal times up no end. I always seemed to 'forget' to close the back door at mealtimes no matter how many times I was reminded.

Strangely enough, for a few weeks that summer Twink stopped visiting us at meal times. I think he was as sick of the bloody luncheon meat as the rest of us.

The last week before we went back to school, I had a religious experience. Well I had an experience of a sort, concerning a few religious people. Melanie's older sister Susan had a friend called Jane (you may remember her from the last book, she was responsible for me getting kicked out of my shed after an experience with a Ouija board), and Jane and her older sister belonged to a free church on our estate. They were involved with a youth group that would take some of the younger kids on trips out in the church van. One day she told me that the church were taking some kids on a trip out to the beach after tea. She said they were going to light a bonfire on the sand after dark and roast some spuds and sing a few songs. She invited me and Melanie to go along. We quite fancied a trip out after dark so we asked our parents. They didn't mind one bit, after all, no children ever came to any harm in a religious group, did they? They'd obviously never heard of the Moonies.

We turned up in the church car park at six o clock that night, we were very excited to be going. The excitement waned a little when we saw the transport, it was a VW camper van, a bit like the Scooby Doo Mystery Mobile. It wasn't so much the van that was the problem, rather the amount of people that had to fit in it.

I think the church must have been giving out rewards to the members for every kid they managed to drag along. There must have been forty of us. It took about an hour to fold us all up and get us in, it was complete madness. The biggest kids got the seats and had to sit on each other's knees three kids high, the medium size kids got to be folded up on the floor and in the footwells and the smallest kids (including me and Melanie) had to go doubled up in the back. I think the two very smallest might have been on the parcel shelf.

When everyone was in and the doors had been welded shut to keep us from falling out, we set off. It was agony, it was cramped, painful and hard to breathe. Every time we went around a bend we all got pushed to one side until the kids against the doors were begging for mercy. At least it wasn't that far to the beach, after about half an hour (that felt like half a week) we arrived. We had to be lifted out one by one and lain out on the grass in a row until we got the feeling back in our legs. When we could move again we were herded onto the beach where some of the church people were busy lighting a bonfire. As bonfires go it was more of a small campfire but they threw some potatoes on it and got some marshmallows on sticks ready. There was no way I was going to eat anything though. With my travel sickness, if I threw up on the way home in that confined space I would be the least popular person on the planet.

After we were sitting round the fire, somebody with a beard (I think it was a man) pulled out a guitar and started singing Amazing Grace, encouraging us all to join in. I was just thinking how much my mother would enjoy this when the singing stopped abruptly. We were then asked to pray for all of Gods wonderful creatures from the smallest to the biggest. Then, one by one, the leader went around the group, asking us to tell our stories about the first time God had spoken to us. What was I supposed to say? Nobody ever spoke to me very much, even in my family and I certainly had never heard from God. When it got to my turn I just sat there, dumbstruck, forty pairs of eyes were watching me sweat. The leader thought I was just being shy and kept badgering me to 'share'. I had nothing, I was tempted to say he had first spoken to me that night in the back of the van.

"He told me to report you lot of nutters to the police for dangerous driving."

I was saved from making some sort of rubbish up by an ear- splitting shriek. One of the other leaders, a hippy looking girl of about twenty, came screaming over the cliffs with a couple of bats fluttering around her. The group went nuts, all the kids with creepy-crawly phobias went running in all directions. The rest of us who weren't scared just sat laughing, while the leader, who five minutes before had been asking us to pray for all God's creatures was busy trying to swat one of said creatures with a marshmallow on a stick. Very Godly I must say.

After that the party broke up and we were all stuffed back into the van for the trip home. Once again, folded in half with Melanie's elbow in my back and someone else's knee up my nose I struggled to breathe. We couldn't tell where we were going, we just knew that the van was swaying left and right alarmingly. I was just hoping that if these people really did have a God, he was keeping an eye on their driving.

CHAPTER THREE

Bedside Manner

I should really have known better than to let Susan and her friends drag me off for a religious experience. The year before they had joined the St Johns Ambulance Brigade and after a few months they convinced me that it would be a good idea if I joined as well. I wasn't keen at first as I was no good with that sort of thing, for one thing I couldn't stand the sight of blood. But they persuaded me by telling me there was a weekend trip to London coming up and if I joined I would be able to go as well, I only had to pay a bit for my place on the coach. Never one to pass up a chance to get away I agreed.

They took me with them to a meeting and to introduce me to the woman in charge. She was called a Captain or Major or some such thing and she was very bossy. She started by using me as a 'patient' for the others to practice on, she told them all in turn to take my pulse. One by one they took my wrist and started pressing on it with their fingers, then one by one they all said they couldn't find a pulse. The bossy woman tutted at them all then she took my wrist, she messed around for ages and then she said she couldn't find one either which probably meant that I was dead.

I was pretty sure she was wrong but straight away I was a bit wary of these people. If they couldn't tell a dead person from a living one I couldn't see how they would be much good in an emergency. Eventually she said she thought she could feel a faint pulse and told me I must be a bit odd. I could have said the same thing to her but I was too polite.

After the pulse taking we moved on to learning how to bandage people up. Half an hour later we looked like a room full of mummies. We had a break after that for some tea and biscuits, I liked that bit, then we had a lecture about broken bones and fractures, it was riveting. Thankfully, after that we could leave.

Susan was bugging me to tell her what I thought. I told her I didn't like it but again she reminded me about the London trip so I agreed to join. A week later when I got my uniform I wished I hadn't, it was hideous. It was much worse than the one I had worn when I was in the Brownies. It was grey, knee length and a bit like the overall my Aunty Dolly wore when she went to work as a cleaner. To top it off it had a jaunty little white nurse's hat that I had to perch on the top of my head. When my parents said how smart I looked I knew I had made a big mistake. Still, there was a free trip coming up so I thought I could stick it out until then. Once I'd had my holiday I would quit.

The next few weeks were some of the most boring of my life. I had no interest in nursing, I didn't know what the hell I was doing and as far as I could tell neither did anyone else. They were all as useless as me and they'd been going for ages. When they bandaged people up they put the bandages on so tight that they cut their circulation off. They choked the C.P.R doll when they were supposed to be doing mouth to mouth resuscitation, added to that, they still couldn't find my pulse. I certainly wouldn't have wanted any of this lot around if I was in an accident, they'd end up making things ten times worse.

One week they showed us a film of a motorcycle accident, it was supposed to inform us what to do if we ever came across one. I still don't know what to do as the minute the motorcycle crashed I came over all funny and had to run to the toilet, I wouldn't come out until it was over. That didn't go down at all well with the bossy woman. I think she would have asked me to leave but I'd already paid for my seat on the coach.

When the weekend of the trip came around we boarded the coach bright and early. My mother had packed me some meat paste sandwiches for the trip, no expense spared there. It took hours to get to London, we seemed to stop at every service station so that somebody could go to the toilet. By the time we arrived it was tea time. We were staying in a hotel somewhere in Bayswater and four if us were sharing a room.

I'd like to say I had a good time but I can't remember any of it so I don't think I can have. We were dragged round big medical demonstrations for two days where lots of people were laying around pretending they'd all had accidents. At least they got to sit down. We never got to go sightseeing, I didn't even see Buckingham Palace. The only two things I remember clearly are getting locked out of my hotel room and having to go down to reception in my pajamas. Then a quick half hour trip to the grounds of Windsor Castle. The Queen wasn't even in.

While we were there we met a French boy who thought our Yorkshire accents were sophisticated. Either he was lying his head off or he was a simpleton, it was hard to tell because he only knew a few words of English. The best I could do in French was ask what time it was and tell him to shut the door.

I was glad when it was time to get back on the bus and go home, I couldn't believe I'd put myself through all those weeks of boredom for that. Eight hours later we were back home again, what a waste of a weekend.

My parents wanted to know what I'd learned while I was there, they were still hoping I would take up nursing so I could look after them in their old age. I told them the only useful thing I'd learned was to never leave your hotel room without your key, especially if you were only wearing pajamas.

CHAPTER FOUR

The Dreaded Day Dawns

It was finally here. The day that I had been dreading for the last six months, my first taste of High School. I woke up that morning, the first week in September, with a sick feeling in my stomach. I would have given anything not to have to go, I wasn't the only one. Downstairs my mother was having a fight with my little brother. It was his first day at primary school and he was not happy about it at all. When I went downstairs he was hiding under the table holding his breath while my mother was trying to drag him out by his legs. He was refusing to get dressed and every time my mother attempted to get his pyjamas off him he went into his old routine of going limp and playing dead. This had worked for him in the past but not today. There was no way my mother was going to pass up the chance of getting us both out of the house.

I left them to it and went into the kitchen to eat my morning Weetabix, it was hard to swallow it down as I was so nervous. I ate half and then went back upstairs to put on my new uniform. It was pretty much the same as my old one but with a different coloured tie. The skirt was a bit longer but I didn't mind that as it would hide my legs. In the last few months my legs seemed to me to be growing ever more bandy, they were shaped like bananas. On looking at a recent photograph of me in the garden, my Uncle Malcom had been heard chortling:

"Look at them legs, she couldn't stop a pig in a poke."

I didn't really know what this meant but I was insulted anyway.

Anyway, this morning I had a choice to make, socks or tights? I wanted to be grown up and wear tights but me and my mother had recently had a disagreement over the colour of the tights I was allowed to wear. I wanted 'American Tan' tights like the other girls wore. My mother decided this was stupid as I wasn't American and no English girl had legs that colour, especially in Yorkshire. She picked the colour she thought was more appropriate, this was 'Bone'.

Who the hell wanted to walk around with bone coloured legs? I would look like a dead person. She wouldn't be swayed though and refused to buy anything else, I tried to persuade her I might look healthier with 'Mink or Honey' coloured legs but she was having none of it. It was 'Bone' or nothing.

I decided to give the bone a try and wear them for a couple of weeks before school started, maybe I would get used to them. All thoughts like this went out of the window the minute my cousin Malcom saw them. I turned up at Aunty Dolly's one day wearing them and he went into hysterics. He said I looked like one of those little old ladies that had their legs wrapped up in bandages. Charming. I took my bone coloured legs home at once, not even stopping for my usual sponge and custard.

I finally decided to go with socks. I had enough to worry about already without being called 'Deadlegs'. If I got saddled with that on my first day I would be stuck with it for the next four years. I collected all the bits and bobs together that I would need for the day and stuffed it all into my schoolbag, praying there wouldn't be any P.E on the first day. I didn't want to be flashing my bandy legs around before anyone got to know me.

Melanie was also extremely nervous about P.E. but for a different reason. We had been told that after the lesson we would have to use communal showers with all the other girls. We were both terrified at this thought. I had never been naked in front of anyone since I was a baby, my mother frowned upon any kind of nudity. Every morning she got dressed under her dressing gown without flashing so much of an inch of flesh. It was like some mad magic trick. It can't have been easy either, given the massive 'All in One' and the copious amounts of talcum powder. When we were in the bathroom, the door had to be locked at all times so that nobody could walk in and catch you without everything covered up. I wished she had been that concerned when I was little and she had trailed half the neighbourhood past while I sat in the tin bath in the living room. All I had were a few pathetic bubbles to protect my modesty.

Melanie was scared of P.E because of her vest. Despite wishing and hoping for her boobs to sprout before we started school, she remained as flat as an eight year old boy. She was terrified she would be the only one still wearing a vest and would get picked on. She had considered wearing a bra and stuffing it with socks but that wouldn't save her in the showers. It would make things worse.

It would be another two years before her boobs popped up but when they did make an appearance it was astonishing. They appeared overnight and they didn't know when to stop growing, she ended up with a bosom much too large for her tiny frame. Then she hated them and wanted smaller ones, we were never happy with our lot. I ended up with normal size ones I suppose, but to this day I am envious of women who can go on a trampoline without clutching their chest as they bounce up and down.

Anyway, I went back downstairs to wait for Melanie to call for me. We were going to walk to school with her sister Susan, who was just starting her last year there. We had both been warned that on no account were we to do anything that might show her up. I had a feeling she might be disappointed there.

Meanwhile, my mother was still wrestling with my brother, whose face by now was a fetching shade of purple. Come to think of it, so was hers, she was getting madder by the minute. I had always sensed when enough was enough but my brother didn't seem to have inherited this sense. He would keep going, pushing and pushing her until she went nuclear. Eventually, by sitting on him she finally managed to get his clothes on him but he was refusing to eat or drink anything.

"Go bloody hungry then."

Was her motherly response to this.

At this point, Melanie knocked on the door so I left my mother wrestling him into his anorak and went off into my nightmare. I wanted to hold my breath and sit under the table as well but I don't think that would have gone down at all well.

We didn't talk much on the way there, Melanie looked even more nervous than me and was really pale. In the distance, we could hear my mother's sweet voice bellowing at my brother to:

"Get up off the floor you bloody idiot and get through them gates."

I felt really sorry for him. He had never been allowed past the garden gate and never allowed to play with the other kids as my mother considered them 'too rough'. I think he had become institutionalised. It took months before he would go to school without a fight and the neighbours became accustomed to the sight of him being dragged past their kitchen windows every morning by his legs. My mother was always being called into school because the teachers couldn't get him to join in with anything. He would sit by the door all day waiting for his chance to go home. He must have felt bad if he would rather stay home with my mother.

In the end, the day I had been dreading didn't turn out to be so bad. At first, everyone stayed in their own groups, with the different junior schools sticking together. There was much eying each other up and down which made me exceedingly thankful that I had left my bone coloured legs at home. We were split up into different classes and sent to our year tutors, luckily, me and Melanie stayed together for now. Our year tutor was called Mr Gray and he seemed more nervous than we were. He was a skinny little man in his thirties with long hair and a beard and spoke really quietly. He told us he would be taking some of us for English as well as being our year tutor. Then he took the register, passed out a load of timetables and sent us on our way.

Finding our way around that first day was a nightmare. Every lesson seemed to be in a different building miles away. We were all late for every lesson that first couple of days as we hadn't a clue where we were going. Some people plucked up the courage to ask the older kids for directions but that just made things worse as they all took great delight in sending us in the opposite direction.

It was a relief for me and Melanie when we found ourselves in the last class of the day, geography. We took out our new books and got on with the lesson, filling out charts and compiling graphs. It was almost the end of the lesson when the teacher asked who we were. It turned out we were in the completely wrong class and should have been next door. We were bundled off to explain to the proper teacher why we had missed the first lesson. I don't know why she had to roll her eyes like that, it was an easy mistake to make.

After that, thank god, it was finally time to leave. We had survived our first day and also, we hadn't embarrassed Susan at all. Still, there was plenty of time for that.

On arrival at home I was greeted by stony silence, my mother and my brother were both having a major sulk. Apparently, he had come home for his dinner refusing point blank to have anything to do with school and there had been a repeat performance of the morning's shenanigans. My mother was threatening him that there had better not be any nonsense the next morning. She hadn't seen anything yet.

When my poor dad got home from work he was immediately confronted by my mother yapping in one ear, telling him to do something about his son. In the other ear, my brother was filling him in about his treatment that day with particular reference to the pulling of his legs. He managed to get free for a minute later on to ask how my day went. I told him it was ok. Even if it hadn't have been I would have kept quiet, he had enough to deal with.

That night I was kept busy covering all my new exercise books with wallpaper. For the last few years we had been encouraged to do this to save our books from wearing out before we had finished writing in them. I was always too embarrassed to use wallpaper from our house. I didn't want people finding out about my dad's strange decorating tastes so I would beg scraps off Melanie's dad or my Aunty Dolly. By the next year, the teachers would be a bit more lenient and allow us to cover our books with pictures of our favourite pop stars. I'm ashamed to say, most of mine were covered by pictures of the Bay City Rollers. At that moment in time though I was still saving myself for David Cassidy. My bedroom walls were covered in his pictures and I would run home from school early every week to watch the Partridge Family. I was convinced that one day he would spot me in a crowd and decide that this much younger, slightly spotty, person with legs the colour of bone was born to be the future Mrs Cassidy. He would whisk me off to California where I would have American Tan legs for real. Me and a couple of million others.

The next few weeks went quickly. We all found our way around eventually and the separate groups of kids began to mingle. New friends were being made and everyone mostly got on ok.

My mother and brother continued their daily fights for many weeks to come. I became accustomed to eating my Weetabix every morning to the soundtrack of tantrums, hysterical screaming, crying and pleading.

And that was just my mother.

CHAPTER FIVE

Hitler and the Disappearing Toupee

If I'd thought we had some strange teachers at my last school, they were nothing compared to the ones at this new school. Most of them seemed to have no interest in teaching at all, they would throw some books at us, tell us which bits to read and then put their feet up to read the paper before escaping to the pub at lunch time. They always came back smelling of booze. It was common knowledge among the staff and the pupils that Mrs Miller, the P.E teacher was having an affair with Mr Grayson, the geography teacher. Everybody knew about it. Countless times they had been caught by pupils in the gym changing rooms, engaging in a bit of out of hours P.E. They didn't care, neither did anyone else (with the exception of Mr Miller had he known about it).

Mrs Willoughby, the cookery teacher spent more time decorating her face than she spent decorating cakes. She was a big fan of blue eyeshadow, also she was orange, this was a fascinating combination when she added the shimmery pale pink lipstick. Every half an hour she would whip out her make up bag to redo her face, adding a bit more orange powder where necessary and topping up the blue eyeshadow. She also had a hairdo that wouldn't have moved in a hurricane, it was solid. She wore so much hairspray that I used to worry her head would catch fire when she was peering into the oven.

One lunchtime when the weather was really hot she took herself off to the far side of the hockey field for a spot of topless sunbathing. Practically every boy (and every male teacher) in the school went for a peek that day, also Miss Hymer strolled by a lot but more on her later. She must have known they were all spying on her but she didn't care. She thought she was the bee's knees, even though she was no spring chicken, she must have been knocking forty. That was practically a dinosaur to us kids in those days, we thought twenty-five was middle aged.

Not long after we had started cookery classes we were roped in to make nibbles for some function the school was giving for god knows who. All we knew was that we weren't invited. Mrs Willoughby, ever the inventive cook, decided what was called for was about a thousand sausage rolls. She slapped half a stone of sausagemeat onto the table and told us to get stuck in. For two hours we slaved away, making pastry and rolling it around bits of fatty sausagemeat. At last we nearly had enough, I put my last two trays into the oven and went to wash up. When I went back twenty minutes later to get my crispy, golden sausage rolls out of the oven they were gone. Puzzled, I asked if anyone had taken them out but everyone said no. By this time Mrs Willoughby was doing a count and asked where my last two trays were. I had to admit I didn't know, they'd vanished. She immediately started shouting for everyone to look around for the missing sausage rolls but no one could find them.

We looked everywhere but they were nowhere to be seen. Finally, she asked me to tell the truth, had I eaten them?

What? Did she seriously think I had just stuffed forty -eight sausage rolls, red hot from the oven into my mouth? I vigorously denied this and some of the other kids backed me up, they had seen me washing up after putting the trays in the oven. In the end, it was one of life's mysteries, we never found out what had happened to them. I think there must have been a black hole in the back of the oven that swallowed them up.

Mrs Willoughby never let me live it down though. For the rest of my time there she would have little sarcastic digs at me every time we had cookery lessons. She would tell the other kids:

"Don't let her put anything in the oven, we might never see it again."

I would have liked to have shoved her head in the oven, blue eyeshadow and all.

Years later, my own daughter was about to start high school and the new headmistress came around to visit all the parents at home to talk about any concerns we might have. You can imagine my shock when I opened my front door to find Mrs Willoughby on my doorstep, orange face and blue eyeshadow resplendent.

My first thought was:

"Bloody hell, she's still looking for those sausage rolls."

My daughter later told me that all the kids made fun of Mrs Willoughby because, still desperately trying to hang on to her youth after all these years she had taken to wearing push up bras. Unfortunately, she pushed her boobs up so high that she created a third boob in the middle of the other two. My daughter said it was fascinating, I just thought it was nice that she was entertaining a whole new generation.

The teacher we were all the most afraid of at my new school was Mr Harram, who taught us German.

He was terrifying, he was one of only a few teachers who took his lessons seriously, really seriously. He did not possess one iota of a sense of humour and could turn you to stone with one glance. The girls would literally shake with fear standing in line outside the classroom and even the cockiest, most boisterous boys were like timid little mice in his class. I don't know why he was so terrifying, I don't remember him hitting any of us, he didn't need to. Because we were so scared of him we always did really well in his classes, in tests we mostly got twenty out of twenty right every time. We all called him Hitler, but only after we were well away from his classroom.

One of our first lessons with him was learning the German names for our families. He told us 'Mother and Father' in German was 'Mutter und Varter' (pronounced Farter) and then said the first person to laugh when we had to say it out loud would be made an example of. Now normally, a bunch of twelve and thirteen year old kids having to say 'farter' would produce the odd giggle. Not in this class, we recited it as if we were at a funeral, we were so scared he might think we were laughing.

One lesson a few weeks later involved the word "schmutzig." I can't remember what it means but I will never forget the word as long as I live. Whenever we were given a new word to master, we had to stand up one by one and repeat the word with the proper pronunciation. On this day, a few of the other kids stood up and said it correctly, then it was my turn. I stood up with quaking knees, Mr Harram's eyes boring into me.

"Schmutzig." I said.

"What did you say girl?" asked Mr Harram.

"Schmutzig", I repeated.

"AGAIN." roared Mr Harram.

"Schmutzig." (I was petrified now).

"What is wrong with you girl?" he screamed "Say it properly."

I tried again.

"Schmutzig."

It didn't matter how many times he told me to repeat it, I couldn't make it sound any different. I didn't know what he wanted from me, as far as I could tell I was pronouncing it the same way as everyone else. On and on it went.

"Schmutzig."

"AGAIN."

"Schmutzig."

"AGAIN."

I was seriously thinking of doing a runner now, it was like being trapped in a nightmare. I knew the other kids were desperately trying to hold their laughter in, some of them were turning pink and trembling but no one dared to even snigger. After about two dozen more 'Schmutzigs' he gave up.

"Sit down girl, you're a disgrace." he bellowed.

It was over, I almost fell into my seat, my legs were that weak. I never did find out what his trouble was, everyone said my 'Schmutzigs' sounded the same as everyone else's. He was obviously hearing something different. I was so relieved at the end of that first year when I could drop German forever and never have to see Mr Harram again.

Why couldn't we be learning French instead, I had always enjoyed French at my junior school. There, we had a proper French teacher, I mean he was actually French, he was from France. His name was Mr Bouffet and he was really nice, he would speak to us in French and we would answer in French as best we could. One day we had to translate some French paragraphs into English and each write a bit on the blackboard. Melanie was very embarrassed when she made a mistake in her translation and invited us all for a tour around the 'pubic' gardens.

Mr Bouffet was almost bald, he had a few strands combed over the top of his head but that was all. One day he turned up at school wearing the biggest, blackest toupee we had ever seen on the top of his head. It looked like he had a big black cat sitting on his head. He walked into the classroom and we all just sat, open mouthed, no one said anything and Mr Bouffet just carried on as usual. He said his usual 'Good morning' in French and we all answered him, waiting to see if he would mention the small animal on his head. Maybe it was a joke.

For the rest of the lesson he never mentioned it and neither did we. We all filed out at the end of the lesson, half expecting him to whip it off and start laughing but he didn't. The next time we had a French lesson it was still there and he still never mentioned it. This went on for weeks and then months. Obviously, it wasn't a joke, he really was going to carry on wearing it. Eventually, we got used to it and we didn't really notice it any more. Then, about a year later, he turned up without it, only now he was balder than he had been before he'd started wearing it. Again, he didn't mention anything, and neither did we. I wonder if the other teachers ignored it like we did. Maybe he thought none of us had noticed anything different.

Who knows? All I remember, apart from the toupee, was that he was a really good teacher. I never took French lessons again after the age of twelve so it's a credit to him that I can still, to this day speak French. As long as I only have to ask what time it is, tell you to close the door, or ask for an ice cream.

Once we got into the swing of things at our new school we were fine. The only lesson we really dreaded (apart from German) was P.E. We only had the adulteress Mrs Miller for one lesson a week, for the other lesson we had Miss Hymer. The first time we met her we thought she was a man, she certainly looked like one. She had short grey hair and wore men's tracksuits all the time, not just for P.E lessons. I was thinking back to my younger days spent reading Famous Five books, George the tomboy had been my idol. I figured this was probably how George had turned out.

Miss Hymer had a very annoying habit of following us into the showers. We were all still far too shy to take naked showers all together so we figured out a routine for getting out of it. We wrapped our towels around us, then ran into the showers and stuck our heads under the water before running out again. Miss Hymer made it her job to ensure we were taking proper showers. She would pop up just as we got one leg into the shower area and try to pull our towels off, she was very determined I must say.

She also made sure that we wore as little as possible when doing P.E lessons. In the middle of winter, she would make us run around the hockey pitch in the snow and ice, wearing little hockey skirts and vests. The other teachers would let you get well wrapped up when it was cold but not Miss Hymer.

There is no pain like having your shin whacked by a hockey stick when it's already freezing. Luckily, Miss Hymer was always on hand to give your leg a good rub if it happened to you. It always seemed to go on far longer than was necessary though.

It was almost as if she was enjoying it.

CHAPTER SIX

Avon Calling

My mother was keeping herself busy now she had a bit more spare time. She had become an Avon lady, along with half the other women on our estate. As soon as the new catalogues were delivered there would be a free for all to see who could get to the customers first. There were more than a few confrontations in the streets between angry women brandishing catalogues and free samples. Every friend and neighbour would be harassed into buying something. My Aunty Dolly would always buy something just to stop the nagging and now that Janice was working she would be badgered into buying bubble bath or talcum powder.

Poor Joan next door was also held to ransom every month or so when ordering time came around. She always bought something small, just to get my mother out of her kitchen.

My dad wasn't happy about my mother's little enterprise at all. He thought everyone would be talking about him and thinking he must have sent his wife out door knocking because he couldn't provide for his family. It caused many a whispered argument in the kitchen when she first started trying to sell the stuff. Not that she ever made any money anyway, she got more doors slammed in her face than the Jehovah's Witnesses that came round every Sunday. Incidentally, my dad always got stuck with these people, he wasn't at all religious and had no time for them at all but he was too polite to tell them that. Every Sunday morning, he would be on the front doorstep for ages and would always come back in with an armful of pamphlets. The rest of us would be laughing like drains eating our breakfast while his went cold.

Anyway, the little bit of money my mother earned was spent on things for herself from the catalogue so she never actually made anything. It meant our bathroom shelf was always full to bursting with various bottles of smelly stuff. My dad used to complain that there was no room for his razor and his Brylcreem.

What really drove him mad though, was when she would take my little brother out Avon collecting with her. She did this in the school holidays and also whenever she couldn't get him to go to school. He was a lot better than he had been but he still hated school. My dad was horrified by this, he didn't think a boy had any business getting involved with make-up and women's things. I don't know why he was so concerned, it wasn't as if she was using my brother to model the products and he has never since shown any interest in cosmetics. As far as I am aware.

She was always trying to involve my brother in her interests, much to my dad's distress. The day he came home from work and found him knitting was an interesting one. I thought he was going to have a stroke, what would he do if the neighbours found out about this one. I sometimes thought he must be on edge all day while he was at work, wondering what my mother was up to now that might attract attention and cause the neighbours to talk about us. He dragged my brother's knitting away from him and told him to get outside and kick a ball, ignoring his protests that he had made him drop his stitches.

My brother just did whatever my mother told him. He had tried to rebel up to the age of about three but she had gradually worn him down and now he just went along with her for an easy life.

He was a very nervous child. I put this down to his early years spent on his own all day with my mother but I must confess (guiltily) that I may have had something to do with this. He was scared of everything and it used to get on my nerves because I had never been like that and I was a girl. One thing that terrified him was the music from Dr Who. Every time the programme started he would run shrieking from the room, hands over his ears, looking for somewhere to hide. After months of this I got fed up, I liked Dr Who and I was fed up of him disrupting my viewing pleasure. Whenever he was getting on my nerves I would just start doing the theme tune in a high voice and that was enough to send him running for the hills.

I also had another form of torture. I would ask him to put a record on my little record player for me and he would do this really carefully. He would pick up the arm with the needle on the end and oh so carefully place it onto the edge of the record. Just as he had nearly managed it and I could see how hard he was concentrating I would shout:

"BANG!"

He would leap about three feet in the air and practically wet himself. I never tired of this and for some reason he never expected it, I got him every time.

Another thing that terrified him was moths. If he ever went to bed and there was a moth fluttering around his room the whole neighbourhood knew about it. You would think there was a man- eating lion in there for all the noise that went on. My mother was the same with spiders, they were a right pair, its a good job they never went camping.

Over the years my parents had never got any better at the social niceties. They would still turn up at people's houses uninvited as they had always done. Didn't matter if the people had something going on or were sitting down to eat, my parents would barge in, under the impression that everyone was pleased to see them. When I was small I could forgive this as we had no telephones to arrange things but now they had no excuse. They were just clueless. They would meet people on holiday and have a nice week with them (they thought). When it was time to go home they would always ask for their new friends' address so they could send Christmas cards, I would have given a fake address but these poor fools probably thought there was no harm in it.

What they didn't know was that they would be stalked by my parents for the rest of their days. As soon as they returned home my mother would start writing them letters telling them all her news, (which was all invented). She would expect a reply and when she got one she would immediately write another letter. Before the poor people knew what had happened they were pen friends with my mother.

She would find out when their birthdays were and send them little gifts (usually Avon free samples). She always expected a gift back and made sure they knew when her birthday was. To this day, she is still writing to people she met thirty years ago, who are no doubt by now regretting the day they ever booked a week in bloody Bournemouth.

They once met a couple on holiday who, by an amazing coincidence (according to my mother) lived on the edge of our town. These poor people were subjected to the letter writing and were soon conscripted into my mother's pen pal club. Even worse though, was the time my parents decided to surprise them by turning up unannounced on their doorstep on Boxing Day. Can you imagine the faces on these people when they opened their door to find my mother, father, and brother on the doorstep? I had left home by then but I would have refused to go anyway. I had been humiliated too many times when I was small, dragged along to gatecrash various parties to which we hadn't been invited. If I, even at that age had been able to see the horror in people's eyes when confronted by us, why couldn't they?

Is there any wonder I spent so many years convinced I was adopted?

Over the years, even after she was widowed my mother has kept up the writing, even though a lot of her pen friends have stopped answering her. She was badgering one of them for months, writing letter after letter and getting no reply until, one day she got a letter to tell her the person had died. It was from whoever had bought this lady's' house, I think she was fed up of seeing all these letters coming through the door. On hearing the news my mother told me:

"Enid's dead."

I said that was a shame (while secretly thinking Enid was probably faking her own death to get a break).

"That'll be why she hasn't written." she said.
I said she was probably right about that one.

Poor Enid would be free now, no more being forced to be a pen pal. That was the only excuse my mother would accept for not writing back – death.

CHAPTER SEVEN

Feeling Lucky

The rest of 1973 was a very funny time for me, not so much for my brother. One afternoon I came home from school at four o clock to find a surprise waiting. It was a little black puppy about three months old. Apparently, a woman my mother had got talking to at the shops had recently had a litter of puppies, well, not the woman herself obviously, I mean her dog had recently had puppies. She had found homes for them all except one. She was stuck with the last one and if no one took it in the next couple of days she was going to take it to the Dogs Home. My mother decided what our madhouse really needed was a dog and so she agreed to take it home.

She called it Lucky, as if she hadn't happened to meet this woman, the pup's luck would have run out.

Now this wasn't our first dog, we had a dog that was already around when I was born but she was long gone. Since then we had owned quite a few dogs, of all shapes and sizes. None of them lasted very long, sooner or later they would do something to annoy my mother and that would be it. We would come home to find our latest dog had 'gone to the farm'. Over the years all our dogs had ended up at this farm, a couple of cats had also gone there, as well as my brother's hamster and the rabbit that none of us ever wanted to clean out. For a few years when I was younger I fully expected that one day a farmer would roll up in his tractor and I would be whisked away to the farm. At least I would have been able to see all my old pets.

I had learnt over the years not to get attached to any of the pets that my mother brought home as I knew they probably wouldn't be around for long. I suspected this new one wouldn't be any different.

This one was a cute little thing, all black and shiny and with very big feet, a sign that it was probably going to get a lot bigger. I say 'it' as at this stage I didn't know if Lucky was a he or a she. I enquired as to what sex Lucky was, only to be met with a blank look from my mother, she hadn't bothered to ask, she said. We tipped Lucky upside down and had a poke about, coming to the conclusion that Lucky was a little boy. I asked what type of dog he was but my mother didn't know that either. She said he was probably just a mongrel but he looked like he had a lot of Labrador in him.

I was sent to the shop to scrounge a cardboard box for him to sleep in while my mother rummaged around in the airing cupboard for some old towels he could use for bedding. When my dad came home to find a strange dog in the corner, he just shook his head, rolled his eyes and let out a big sigh. He had been here before.

During the next few weeks Lucky grew at an alarming rate, we came to think he had some German Shepherd in his blood as well. He quickly outgrew his cardboard box (as well as eating half of it) and I had to keep running to the shop for bigger and bigger ones. Eventually there weren't any big enough so from then on, he just slept on his blankets in the corner.

Now Labradors and German Shepherds are supposed to be intelligent dogs. Lucky was the stupidest dog I'd ever met. He was incapable of mastering the simplest of tasks. Ask him to sit and he would just stand there looking confused, throw him a ball to play fetch and he would just take it off and eat it. He was useless. There was one thing he was good at though, he could sing.

This came to light one evening while my mother was giving the regular teatime concert through the kitchen window. She was in fine voice as usual, murdering every note and shrieking on all the high bits. I was outside playing double ball against the shed wall when all of a sudden, she began to howl. Now this was a new one on me, I had heard many strange noises come out of that woman over the years but I couldn't recall hearing her howl before. It sounded as if she was throwing her voice at the same time, I could still hear the usual strangled cat noise but the howling was happening at the same time, it was very strange. I went inside to see how she was doing it and then I realised what I'd been hearing. Lucky was sitting in the kitchen while my mother was throwing the pots and pans around and warbling, he had his head thrown back and he was howling as if his life depended on it. It was so funny. My mother thought it was great, she had someone to accompany her when Joan next door wasn't around.

When my dad came home she showed him her new act. He laughed along with the rest of us but I could see the worry in his eyes, people would hear this and talk about us. He lived in fear of being talked about. Did he not realise that people had been talking about us for years.

After that, Lucky and my mother put on a production every night at half past five. Sometimes,

Joan would join in and the street would be ringing with the sound of the three of them, shrieking, warbling and howling. Every kid in the street would turn up and sit under the kitchen window laughing until they cried. They had been doing this for the last few years anyway, listening to my mother but now she was taking it to a whole new level. It's a wonder we never got a visit from the police. Oddly enough, Lucky would only sing along with my mother, he wouldn't duet with anyone else. If we tried to get him singing he would just give us the usual confused look. I think my mother must have had that certain pitch that only dogs can hear. Unless we had got it all wrong and instead of joining in with her he was howling for her to please stop. If so I knew how he felt.

When Lucky was about six months old he suddenly fell in love (or rather lust) with my little brother. Whenever he entered the room Lucky would instantly jump on him, wrapping his front paws around his waist while vigorously humping his legs. By this time, he was as big as my brother so he couldn't get away. If he tried to run, Lucky would just knock him down and carry on humping his head or whatever part of him he could get to. My mother was horrified. She would jump on the dog, trying to prise him away from the object of his affection while my brother screamed like a banshee and tried to climb out from underneath the pair of them. I thought this was the funniest thing I had ever seen. She would scream at me to come and help but I would be too busy rolling around on the floor trying to get my breath.

Lucky never assaulted any of the rest of the family, he never really bothered visitors either, apart from being a bit personal with his sniffing habits. We could have walked past him wearing the doggy equivalent of stockings and suspenders and he wouldn't have batted an eyelid. But one glimpse of my brother in his duffle coat and all hell would let loose. Lucky would be on him in an instant, while my mother would be behind them both, brandishing a yardbrush and screaming at the dog to:

"Put him down, you bloody great pervert."

I think my brother's sudden change of heart concerning going to school had a lot to do with Lucky and his amorous intentions. I think he figured he was safer at school. It was a bit ironic really, he was going to school to escape sexual harassment, while I went to school and faced the same thing every second P.E lesson.

Not long after that, Lucky's luck ran out. My mother put up for him for a while longer but just after Christmas he crossed the line. All the humping must have given him an appetite and, when my mother's back was turned he sneaked into the kitchen and ate the joint of beef she had been cooking for Sunday dinner. That was the last straw she said. A few days later we came home from school to find Lucky had gone the same way as all the others. He was at the 'farm'. My brother was very relieved, he could walk around the house without looking over his shoulder every two minutes now.

I felt bad for Lucky, he was a stupid oversexed mongrel but he deserved better. At least at the farm he would have all our other pets to play with.

CHAPTER EIGHT

Who Turned the Lights Out?

1974 was a very strange year. Just after Christmas the miners went on strike for better wages and for the next three months we had regular blackouts. The government rationed the power so they brought in the three-day week, which meant closing businesses for the other two days to save on power. They also decided to ration the power for the rest of us so we all went through the next three months never knowing when we were going to be plunged into darkness. The local newspaper would print the times when the power was most likely to go off but it still usually took everyone by surprise.

Most times it would go off when my mother was in the middle of cooking the tea. It drove her nuts. She would have the chips frying away in the chip pan, watching the clock and praying the power would last for a bit longer when suddenly everything would go off. That meant that yet again we would be eating half raw chips with luke warm meat pies from the rapidly cooling oven. Usually, by the time we sat down to eat it everything was cold. Luckily, we couldn't see how unappetising it all looked as we were dining by candlelight. It's a wonder more people didn't go down with food poisoning. It was worse for the people queuing up at the fish and chip shop. The lucky few at the front would get hot food, while the people at the back would have to go stumbling home through the darkness with half cooked, cold fish and chips.

No matter how much we tried to prepare my brother for the lights going out, it always frightened him half to death, and the rest of us come to that. It was bad enough being mid-cooking, homework, or whatever else we were doing when the blackness descended, but add to that the sudden shrieking of a hysterical four-and-a-half-year old with a nervous disposition and it really shattered your nerves. We told him time and time again to stay still until we'd got the candles lit (we had them all over the house) but he never did. We would hear things crashing to the ground, ornaments falling over and shouts of pain as he went thrashing around the house in terror screaming and falling over things. My mother would also be screaming:

"Stay where you are you daft sod while I light the bloody candles."

It was a magical time.

Meanwhile, everyone else in the street was in the same boat. Up and down the block you could hear women cursing as they tried to finish feeding their families with no power, shouting for their kids to:

"Fetch the bloody matches."

For the next few months everything was thrown into chaos. The hairdressers at the top of our street was filled most days with women with rollers in their wet hair, sitting under dryers, waiting for the power to come back on.

Because the street lights were off as well, we were all given fluorescent arm bands to wear so that we didn't get run over on the way home from school, being winter it was dark by half past three. It was really eerie walking home in the pitch black, all you could see were the arm bands floating around everywhere with no bodies attached. Some of the boys would take theirs off so they could sneak up on you in the darkness and make you wet yourself.

After the first few weeks the shops all ran out of candles so we were only allowed to light one at a time. Until it had burnt down to the very end we weren't allowed to light another one. This meant going to bed was really fun, my mother would stand at the bottom of the stairs to give me enough light to get to my room, then I would have to fumble around the bathroom and then my bedroom like a blind person.

Because it always went off before the good telly programs started there was nothing to entertain us of an evening. My parents would tell tales of the good old days when nobody had a telly and everyone would gather around the piano for a good old fashioned sing song. Not for the first time I thanked god that we didn't have room for a piano. To pass the time my mother would get a deck of cards out and we would play gin rummy around our one candle, squinting at the cards, until we would all have to go to bed with a migraine. Even if the power stayed on, telly went off at half past ten every night to conserve power.

During the seventies there were always strikes, I remember power strikes, fuel strikes, bread strikes, dustmen's strikes. People would beat each other to death with the last loaf of bread in the shop as everyone went mental stockpiling food. It was mad.

Up and down the country all the grown ups were up in arms, it was all anyone ever talked about and every newspaper was full of all the bad news. I didn't care really, most of it passed me and my friends by. The only thing that annoyed me was when the power went off when I was playing records on my little record player. I played Tiger Feet by Mud all the time as there was a dance that went with it that I was learning. If it went off mid Coronation Street I would get mad as well, I loved Corrie and we watched it religiously in our house (I still do).

Sometimes I would try and read my Jackie magazine by the light of our one candle but I would have to sit so close to it I was in danger of catching fire.

To me and every other teenage girl in Britain, Jackie was our bible. We read it over and over, cutting out the pop stars' pictures for our bedroom walls and poring over the makeup tips. My favourite bit was the problem page with Cathy and Claire. Today's teenagers would find it laughable compared to the problem pages nowadays. It was full of girls asking, 'How do I know if a boy likes me' or 'What can I do about my dandruff', serious stuff in the seventies.

Cathy and Claire would have dropped dead on the spot if they could see what's on most problem pages today, questions about sexually transmitted diseases and different positions. They used to advise us to wait six months before kissing anyone, and then if you did it you had to keep your lips tightly shut.

We used to read our horoscopes as if they were gospel, believing every word of drivel:

"Today you will meet your secret admirer" and "Your luck is about to change."

Mind you mine usually did, for the worse.

Sometimes in Jackie they would print massive posters but split them into three parts. Each week for three weeks you got a different bit, you collected them all and at the end of the three weeks you stuck it all together. The first week you got the legs, the second week you got the middle bit and the third you got the head. My mother didn't know this and went mental when she was glancing through my copy on week two. She demanded to know what the hell kind of magazine would print a poster of Marc Bolan's crotch.

My parents hated it when I went through my T Rex phase, they much preferred David Cassidy. My mother said Marc Bolan was a dirty drug addict, she said that about most pop stars in those days, even if they'd never popped anything stronger than an aspirin. If their hair was too long or their pants were too tight, they were probably on drugs. I had bought the Electric Warrior album when I was eleven and I had the words to all the songs. My parents read the lyrics in disbelief, they kept questioning me:

"What did this mean, what did that mean, and what the hell was a 'Hub Cap Diamond Star Halo?"

How was I supposed to know? I was eleven. I just thought Marc Bolan was dead cool. They would go off, shaking their heads, my mother asking what was wrong with Perry Como.

When Top of the Pops came on every week they would both sit there bewildered. There were a lot of cheesy pop songs in the seventies and my mother was fine with these, she would sit, warbling along with Renee and Renata or Demis Roussos. Whenever the Sweet came on or Slade or any other males wearing glitter and make up she would tut loudly all the way through the songs telling us there must be 'something wrong with them. My dad would sit behind his newspaper avoiding it all until Pans People, the all-girl dance troupe came on in their hotpants and then he would suddenly perk up and appear above the top of the paper.

They both acted as if they were pensioners when in fact they were only in their late thirties. In the sixties at the height of Flower Power they tutted their way through all that as well, even though at that time they were barely thirty. I remember asking for a cowbell when I was about seven as all the older girls were wearing them. My mother said there was no way I was going to be copying those long-haired hippies. Most of these 'hippies' were my parent's age but it passed them by completely. If I was them I would have been walking around in my floaty clothes wearing all the flowers and cowbells I could have got my hands on.

CHAPTER NINE

What Are You Pointing At?

After the miners' strike finished and the power came back on things got back to normal, well as normal as they ever could be in my house. My cousin Janice had left school by now and was training to be a hairdresser. She needed somebody to practice on and, as my mother had never been known to turn down a freebie, she became her 'model'.

Every week she would go off to the college where Janice was training and get her hair done in a 'shampoo and set', Janice would be marked on how well it turned out. This went on for about a year, until Janice had qualified and was working in a proper hairdresser's salon. To pay her back for modelling for her Janice gave her a free hairdo every week after that. I think she came to regret offering this as it carried on every week for the next forty years, my mother never did her own hair again.

We had all settled down into a routine at our new school now and it was starting to feel as if we belonged there. Most of the teachers were very laid back with the exception of Mr Harram, who I have already mentioned. One other exception was Mr Cornwell, who taught us Chemistry. He was about forty and quite big and fit, he didn't like our class much as we were all useless at Chemistry. At least once a week one of us would set something alight with our Bunsen burner or cause a small explosion. One lesson we arrived early and had to sit and wait for him.

The boys were fiddling around with the various bottles of stuff on the tables, passing them around and smelling them. A boy called David somebody held a bottle under my nose:

"Smell that." he said "What does that smell like?"

Stupidly, I took a big sniff.

When I came round, everyone was rolling around laughing, I couldn't hear them as my ears were still ringing. When I composed myself and got up from under the table they told me it was really strong ammonia. Thanks for that.

Just as I got back on my stool the door opened and Mr Cornwell came in. Thankfully he missed my performance and the lesson got under way. I can't remember what we were supposed to be doing but as usual we made a mess of it, Mr Cornwell was fast running out of patience. He had a go at one of the bigger lads called Andrew for doing it all wrong and Andrew had a go back at him. Out of the blue Mr Cornwell hit him round the back of the head. This didn't shock any of us, we had grown up being knocked around and manhandled by teachers since we were in primary school. What happened next shocked us though as Andrew stood up and hit him back. Now this was new. Instantly we all took off our safety goggles to see what would happen next.

Mr Cornwell hit him again, harder, Andrew retaliated by hitting him back again twice as hard. Mr Cornwell snapped, he threw Andrew bodily across the classroom, jars and bottles went flying and there were some most peculiar smells. Andrew came flying back at him, charging like a bull. We were properly enthralled now, we had never seen anything like this before.

They grabbed hold of each other and started to wrestle, each trying to land a punch on the other. Clothes were being ripped, Andrew's jumper ended up pulled over his head, at one point he was trying to strangle Mr Cornwell with his own tie. We were all completely gobsmacked by this time, incidentally, not one of us bothered to call for help. We were far too interested in seeing who won.

After a few more rounds, another teacher passing by heard the commotion and came in. When he saw what was going on he leapt on Andrew and together, he and Mr Cornwell manhandled him off to the headmaster's office.

We didn't see Andrew again for a few weeks after that. When he came back to school he wasn't in our class for Chemistry any more, he was transferred to a different class with a different teacher. After that performance, we all got a bit worried about being taught by Mr Cornwell. Something good came out of it though, we all got a lot better at chemistry.

1974 was the year I really got into the Bay City Rollers. I had seen them on some telly program the year before and went round telling everyone they were going to be famous. When they actually were, nobody remembered me telling them. All my other posters were consigned to the bin and every inch of my bedroom walls were plastered with pictures of them. Most of my friends liked Les and Eric the best but my young heart belonged to Woody.

Looking back now I can't believe how pink my rose coloured specs must have been. Woody, bless him, was the most gormless looking lad ever. If he'd worked in the corner shop nobody would have paid him the least bit attention. Maybe that's why I fell for him, I must have sensed a kindred spirit. He always looked really uncomfortable on telly, as if he didn't really want people looking at him. I swear he used to blush.

That year, practically every teenage girl in the land went mad for the Rollers. We had a uniform of white cropped trousers with tartan sewn on the bottoms, stripey socks and baseball boots. To top it all off you had to be wearing a tartan scarf at all times, we were called the Tartan Army by all the newspapers of the time.

My parents were completely flummaxed by all this. My dad wouldn't be seen out with me in public if I was wearing my tartan. I often heard him complaining to my mother:

"Why can't she just wear a nice dress, she's not even Scottish." My mother would tell him it was just a phase,

"She'll grow out of it." she would tell him

"Remember when she loved the drug addict." Then they would both scream at me to,

"Turn that bloody rubbish down, Shang a Lang isn't even a proper bloody word."

The Rollers had longish hair that was spikey on the top. Teenage boys everywhere cottoned on to the fact that if they copied the haircut, they could convince all these teenage girls that they were the next best thing. It didn't always work but you couldn't blame them for trying.

That summer my parents booked a week's holiday in Scarborough for us and they said that Melanie could come with us. She was a bit nervous about this as she had heard me and Janice talking about all the walking my parents used to make us do, especially when we took Janice with us to Whitby and made her walk miles. Her knees had never been the same since.

I assured her that things were different now. After my brother was born they stopped the marathon walks as he could never keep up with them. It never mattered to them that I couldn't keep up when I was his age, I was dragged along anyway. He had mastered the sitting down protest in a way I never had. When he'd had enough walking, he would just simply sit down wherever he was, usually in the middle of the pavement.

My parents would try to make him get up again but he would just sit there, refusing to move. He knew that my mother would start shouting and trying to drag him along and he also knew that my dad would do anything to avoid people looking at them. My dad would always give in to save himself from the embarrassment of my mother causing a scene and so they would return home or catch a bus. How come I never got away with anything like that?

We stayed in a flat that my parents had rented for the week, it was pretty basic but it was ok because we went out a lot. I think we went to every attraction Scarborough had to offer that week. We did the bucket and spade thing so my brother could see how much fun it was building sandcastles. He didn't like it, he got sand in his eyes. We paddled in the sea so my brother could see what that was like. He didn't like that either, it was too cold. We rode donkeys up the beach so he could see how much fun that could be. He screamed blue murder until my mother took him off poor Blossom. I was beginning to think he wasn't cut out for the seaside.

My dad took hundreds of photos of us that week, well it felt like hundreds. On nearly every one of them, me, Melanie, my mother and my brother are all pointing at things. That was my dad's favourite holiday pose.

"Stand in a line, budge up a bit, now all point at that tree."

We never knew why we were pointing at things, we must have looked like mad people. We would stand there pointing at buildings, ducks, flowers, you name it, we pointed at it.

About halfway through the week we went to some sort of park. All I remember about the actual park was that they had big animals dotted around and the odd dinosaur, all made out of paper mache and painted bright colours. My dad tried to make us all point at one but my brother was scared of it.

There was one attraction where you had to go through a giant whale's mouth to get inside (not a real one, that was paper mache too). I don't remember what was inside it but that doesn't really matter, my mother was the main attraction that day. Inside they had the kind of lighting that made anything white glow in the dark. We were all walking around inside when I noticed people sniggering at us. Now I was quite used to this so I didn't take much notice at first. Then I realised they were all laughing at my mother. The lighting had made her all in one underwear glow in the dark through her dress, she looked like she was walking around in her unmentionables.

When my dad realised what was going in he was mortified. He grabbed my mother and started dragging her towards the exit while at the same time trying to cover her up with his jacket. It was hilarious. I often wondered afterwards if anyone managed to take a photo of her in there. Now that would have been something worth pointing at.

On our last day in Scarborough we went to a model village, that was exciting. My dad thought it was hilarious to take lots of photos of us all standing in the middle of the houses pretending to be giants. We did it to keep him happy though, and yes, you've guessed it, we were pointing.

CHAPTER TEN

Goggle Box

Our family had finally made it into the 20th Century, the year before we had got a coloured telly. Most other families had been watching in colour for ages but we had caught up with them at last. Melanie's was one of the last families to get one, her dad said they wouldn't be getting a new telly until their old black and white set died so it was 1976 before they got one.

Watching in colour was amazing at first, we were amazed by how green the grass looked, we were amazed by how blue the sky looked, we oohed and aahed over how tanned Des O Connor was. We were like cavemen discovering fire. You would have thought we'd never seen the real thing (I mean grass and sky, not Des O Connor, we'd never seen him in real life).

For the first few weeks, until the novelty wore off, we watched it constantly. We watched anything and everything. Eventually, we stopped looking at the test card and just stuck to our usual favourites. Me and my mother and my cousin Janice watched Coronation Street twice a week without fail. We had no videos or Sky+ in those days so if you missed it you missed it, that was that. Mondays and Wednesdays at 7.30 pm, as soon as the familiar trumpet music started (some sort of brass instrument anyway), we were there.

As a family, we mostly watched comedies. My parents loved 'Are You Being Served' which was quite rude for the times. Everybody we knew laughed themselves silly watching Mrs Slocombe talking about her pussy and Mr 'I'm Free' Humphries who was the gayest man ever on telly. Sometimes I thought I got the jokes more than my mother did, she wasn't very streetwise for her age. She once asked what on earth Liberace's wife must think to her husband wearing all that jewelry.

My mother always watched 'Terry and June', they lived in the sort of world she had always wanted to be in. They were terribly middle class, talked posh and called each other 'Darling' every three seconds. Terry would come home from a hard day doing sod all at the office and June would be waiting with his dinner in the oven and a gin and tonic in her hand so he could relax before eating. June wore Crimplene trouser suits and they both played golf, they were a right pair of twits. They never mentioned their kids, I don't think they had any because June was far too posh for hanky panky, and she would have had to take off the trouser suit.

It was as far removed from our life as you could possibly get. My dad cycled home on his pushbike every night, knackered from working in a factory all day. He never drank a gin and tonic in his life and wouldn't have known one end of a golf club from the other. There was no dinner waiting in the oven in our house, just a big pan of chips bubbling away in half a gallon of lard. And I never heard them call each other 'Darling' unless they were being sarcastic. Still, in my mother's mind she was living just like they were and every week she tried to get Janice to copy June's hairdo. Every week she ended up looking more like Terry.

I used to watch Blue Peter every week while I was waiting for my chips, I had been watching it since I was really small. Every episode they would show you how to make something out of crap. I had made pencil holders out of toilet roll tubes, jewellry trays out of washing up liquid bottles and plastic cutlery racks, I made no end of crap. One year me and my mother made an advent crown out of wire coat hangers and tinsel, it held a candle in all four corners. We hung it up and it looked beautiful, until we lit the candles and the whole thing went up in flames.

Everything they showed you how to make needed 'sticky back plastic'. I didn't know what that was or where to get it from and neither did any other kid I ever met. Years later I found out it was just good old fashioned sellotape but they hadn't been allowed to say the brand name. Brilliant, we'd had rolls and rolls of the bloody stuff in the kitchen drawer, my dad used to 'borrow' it from work. They were quite patronising on Blue Peter, they talked as if all of us watching were slightly stupid, and they always told us to get a grown up to help us, even if all we were doing was putting a blob of glue onto a bit of card. Back then glue sniffing was unheard of to us so I don't know why they were so bothered. Eventually, I got tired of being talked down to and I started watching 'Magpie' on the other side. They were cooler on Magpie and didn't treat you like you were a bit slow.

Coronation Street wasn't the only soap we watched back then. we also had 'Crossroads'. This was on about half past six every night and although it wasn't meant to be a comedy it was hysterical. It was set in a motel in Birmingham and it was made so cheaply that the set would fall to bits while the cast were acting. Someone would walk out of a room, slamming a door and the whole wall would sway and wobble. Staircases would fall apart, people would be holding things up hoping we hadn't noticed, and the actors were appalling. The camera would cut to someone and they would be caught completely off guard, either frozen to the spot trying to remember their lines, or chatting away to someone off camera. It was so funny.

But by far and away the best thing on telly in our house in the 1970s were Morcambe and Wise, we loved them, everyone did. Every Christmas the highlight of the whole holidays was The Morcambe and Wise Christmas Special. We would all gather round the telly after Christmas dinner to watch it and it was all anyone talked about for weeks after. One year, Eric Morcambe dressed up as a woman in a long dark wig and we all thought it was my Aunty Dolly on the screen, she wasn't as amused as the rest of us were. I think my best childhood memory is of watching them every Christmas and they still make me smile forty years later. When Eric Morcambe died in the early 1980s it felt like a member of our family had gone.

When we weren't watching telly my parents would play a lot of records on our stereogram, this looked like a sideboard but was actually a record player and radio with big cupboards to hide away all your LP's. That means long playing records to all you babies reading this. My dad loved Shirley Bassey and had all her records even though we'd all been forced to hear my mother murdering her songs over the years. They also played a lot of Frank Sinatra and my mother loved her musicals so we had South Pacific, The Sound of

Music, The King and I and countless others that she could shriek along with, usually when I had friends around. Most of them were used to her by now though, some of them had, over the years been pressed into duetting with her.

My parents didn't really like much of the music I played back then. Everyone my age loved Suzy Quatro, Mud, David Essex, Slade, Gary Glitter (before we knew). The Osmonds were around in those days as well but they were a bit squeaky clean and they were Mormons, my parents thought that must be a cult. When my dad found out that Mormons could have more than one wife he said they must be gluttons for bloody punishment.

Barry White was big back then as well (I don't mean physically), a lot of older ladies liked him a lot. Incidentally, I once went to a funeral where the choice of song going into the church was 'My first, my last, my everything' by Barry White. All I can say in my defense is, you try walking behind a coffin to that song without dancing.

As I said before, my mother liked a lot of the cheesy pop songs of the day and could often be heard caterwauling 'Tie a Yellow Ribbon' or 'Save All Your Kisses for me, usually while trying to do the dance that went with it. She loved all the rubbish from the Eurovision Song Contest, in fact she loved anything that I considered rubbish.

We once had a bit of a get together at our house over Christmas and I was so embarrassed to see her, in a full-length evening gown that looked like my Nanna's curtains, bopping around the living room to 'Remember You're a Womble'.

One group that we both liked (at least until I got fed up of them) was Abba. She would come into my room to pinch my records to play downstairs. All my friends liked Abba when they first came out too, every girl wanted to look like the blonde one Agnetha, and we copied her hair and bright blue eyeshadow. Unfortunately, no matter how much I tried to imitate her I always looked more like Bjorn (the one without the beard).

Today, my mother only listens to really old songs from the 1950s but every day she sits down to watch the repeats of 'Are You Being Served on Sky TV, she must have seen them hundreds of times now but she never gets tired of watching them. Sometimes I think she still doesn't get the jokes.

CHAPTER ELEVEN

My Bubble Has Burst

All through 1974 I was in love with Woody, I played Bay City Rollers records none stop and drove my parent's nuts. At one point even Colin, the man next door was begging me to stop. All his kids were boys so he wasn't going through what most of the other dads were. Towards the end of the year we heard the biggest, most exciting news ever, The Bay City Rollers were coming to our town. They would be playing at our local cinema on the 11th of November, tickets would be £1. I was beside myself at the news, practically every girl in town was, except Janice who called them a load of skinny poofs. She was still into Slade, she had been for years, her heart belonged to Noddy Holder. All her George Best posters had been replaced with ones of Noddy and his massive sideburns.

My parents said there was no way they could afford £1 for a ticket. That was a fortune in those days, that could feed us all for a week. I was heartbroken, what was I going to do? In the end my cousin Malcom took pity on me. He was working now and he said he would lend me the pound until I could afford to pay him back. Bless him, I think he felt a bit guilty for all the judo practice and the Chinese burns he'd given me over the years. Tickets were expected to be sold out instantly so everyone was camping out all night outside the pictures to grab them. Of course, I wasn't allowed to stay out all night but my friend Becky from school was so she sat outside all night wrapped up in a blanket and managed to get us two tickets. Poor Melanie couldn't go to the concert as it would be at night and she wasn't allowed out after dark on her own, but she was never really such a big fan as me anyway. I don't think she was all that bothered really.

I was beside myself with excitement. Every day I checked to make sure my ticket was still there and hadn't been stolen by some mad fan who couldn't get one, or sold on by my mother at a profit. I was crossing the days off until the concert on my calendar (A Bay City Rollers one of course).

This wouldn't be my first concert. The year before I had gone with some of my friends to see Mud playing at the City Hall. The same venue where a few years ago, I myself had graced the stage, country dancing, wearing half a tablecloth. I had bought all of Mud's records and I thought I might get a chance to show off the dance I had been practicing for months.

When we got to the concert and started queuing up outside we bumped into Janice and her friends. She was being unfaithful to Slade for the night by going to see Mud. She was horrified to see me there and warned me to behave, stay in my seat and not to do anything that might embarrass her or she would tell my mother. I told her not to worry, she wouldn't even see me from her seats anyway.

We got inside and the concert got underway, I don't remember much about it so it can't have been that good. The only bit I do remember is that about half way through, some of the audience decided to storm the stage. It looked like fun so me and my friends joined in. We were all pushing and shoving to get to the front, a couple of older girls actually got onto the stage. I managed to get hold of Les Gray the singer (who up close looked as old as my dad) for a couple of seconds before the bouncers intervened and started shoving us all back. This was fun, I was having a great time. Then, over the top of the music, the singing and the bouncers shouting at us, I heard Janice.

"Get back in your seat now and stop making a show of yourself. Just you wait til we get back home, I'm going straight to see your mother."

I took no notice of her. I didn't believe she would really tell on me. I ignored her and went back to pushing and shoving along with everyone else. Suddenly a hand clamped around the back of my neck, at first I thought one of the bouncers was getting a bit heavy handed until I heard the familiar voice in my ear.

"I frigging warned you didn't I? Now get back in that frigging seat before I rip your frigging head off and tell your frigging mother."

Well really, that was a bit uncalled for. Without another frigging word, she dragged me by my neck back to my seat and dumped me unceremoniously into it.

"Now frigging stay there."

I decided I'd better do as she advised, I had no idea she was so strong. She was certainly wasted as a hairdresser, she should have been in security.

At last, after what seemed to be an eternity of waiting, the big day was finally here. All day at school we talked of nothing else. All the girls that were going that night were practically throwing up with excitement, we couldn't wait. After what seemed the longest day ever, the hands on the clock rolled around to four, we were free to go home and get ready for the best night of our lives.

I couldn't eat my tea that night, my stomach was full of butterflies. The concert was supposed to start at 7.45pm, I was going to meet Becky an hour before so we could get in line and find our seats in good time. I went off to catch the bus, it was full of tartan clad teenage girls singing Bay City Rollers songs all the way into town. The poor bus driver must have been going mental with the noise, he certainly seemed to get us all there quickly. As soon as the bus stopped in town I found Becky and we crossed the road to take our places in the queue.

There were hundreds of us, all looking exactly the same and clutching our scarves as if our lives depended on it. There was a photographer from the local paper taking pictures of everyone, it was the biggest thing to hit our town since the Beatles over ten years before. At last, the doors opened and we all stampeded in, ready to meet our idols.

Me and Becky were on the balcony, right at the front so we had a really good view. While we waited, we sang and chanted, some girls were crying already. After about the third rendition of Bye Bye Baby there was movement on the stage, we all held our breath, the curtains opened and there, in all their tartan glory were our heroes. The place went nuts, it was deafening and the vibrations through the floor went from my feet, up through my body and into my head. For a minute, I was a bit worried that the balcony wouldn't take the weight of us all, stomping and banging around. I was scared it would collapse, sending us all hurtling down onto the rest of the fans below. I can't remember what the first song was but it was one of their hits, this was the moment I'd been waiting for.

I don't really know what happened next. Halfway through the next song I suddenly began to feel strange, I couldn't put my finger on what was going on but something was definitely wrong. Then it hit me. They were rubbish!

I know there was a lot of noise but you could still hear them and they sounded awful, this was worse than listening to my mother. And they were half heartedly dancing around the stage as if they really couldn't be bothered. They looked like a lot of silly lads at a school disco. My eyes searched out Woody, my beloved, there he was on the left, he had the same expression my dad got whenever my mother was causing a scene and he just wanted to get away from it all. This was awful.

I looked around at everyone else to see if they felt the same way but they were all crying and screaming, a couple of girls had fainted and the St Johns Ambulance people were trying to get them out. It was proper mass hysteria, so why wasn't I hysterical as well?

I felt like the little kid in the story of The Emperor's New Clothes, was I the only one who could see they were naked (figuratively speaking)? I sneaked a peek at Becky, she was singing along with everyone else and having a great time. I figured I'd better just pretend I was having a great time along with her, maybe it would get better. It didn't.

I think they played for about an hour, it didn't seem very long anyway. Then they shouted goodbye, gave everyone a final wave and then they were gone. Leaving behind a theatre full of sobbing, hysterical, tartan covered girls, holding each other up while crying on each other's shoulders. We all trooped back out again, into the dark and the cold. It was hard to get through the crowds of girls all trying to head for the stage door, there were police waiting outside to stop anyone who had that idea so they were getting even more hysterical now. I just wanted to get home, away from all this madness. Becky had to be home at the same time as me so we tried to head for the bus station. On the way, we were confronted by the sight of Julie, a girl from our class, she was laying down on the road in front of a double decker bus, shouting something. When we got closer we heard what she was shouting. She was demanding to be taken to see Les from the group. She wasn't moving until she got her way and she didn't care if she had to stay there all night.

She didn't. Two big policemen picked her up, one under each armpit, and deposited her at the side of the road where she collapsed in a heap of snot and tears. This was complete madness. Me and Becky said our goodbyes and went off to catch our separate buses home.

When I got home my parents wanted to know all the details.

"What was it like, did you enjoy it?"

I forced a smile and said it was brilliant. I couldn't admit to them that they'd been right all along, I'd been listening to complete rubbish for months. Was this what it was like when you saw your idols in real life? I hadn't felt this bad when I had been to see Mud, but I hadn't been in love with them like I had been with the Rollers.

I lay in bed that night, looking at Woody's gormless face and felt cheated.

"You were supposed to be good" I told him accusingly.

He just looked back at me with his usual blank expression, no help at all.

The next day at school everyone was going on about how great it had all been, on and on they went, all day, talking about every little detail of the big night. I went along with it all, pretending I was just as carried away as they all were, I didn't want to be the odd one out.

For a few more weeks I kept up the charade but slowly, my posters started to come down and I only played the Roller's records when my friends were there. When I saw my cousin Malcom he asked me if it had been worth the pound he'd lent me. I came clean and told him the whole story. He said it was a good thing, it proved I didn't have such bad taste in music as he'd thought. After that, he started lending me some of his LP's by bands that played their own instruments properly and could sing in tune. I never got into any more teeny bopper bands again after that. I moved on to Rod Stewart, his music was miles better and it also meant that all my tartan wasn't wasted.

As a last note: What I didn't know at this time was that my future husband (who I had yet to meet) was also involved in the Bay City Rollers visit to our town. Having left school not long before, he was working for a laundry service and it was his job to go around the hotels in the area picking up the dirty laundry from the rooms. He had to pick up the laundry from the hotel that the band was staying in. That week he made a fortune selling dirty pillow cases to the schoolgirls waiting outside by telling them this was the pillowcase that their favourite Roller had slept on. He also got a few quid by selling half eaten sandwiches from the hotel bins, telling the girls that the teeth marks in them were also made by their favourite.

I think it was his enterprising ways that must have caught me.

CHAPTER TWELVE

Jingle Bells

Christmas 1974 was almost upon us. Slade were back on the radio singing Merry Christmas Everybody, that was good, we hadn't heard it much since last year. We weren't to know then that we would still be hearing it every bloody Christmas for the next forty years (to date).

In our house, we were preparing for the Christmas tree. Every year we put it up on my birthday, the first week in December and every year my dad insisted on getting a real tree. This hadn't been such a bad idea in our old house, we only had a gas fire to keep us warm then. In this house we had central heating, which didn't go well with living plants and trees. Every year we would decorate a lush, green, healthy looking tree, within a week of being in our centrally heated living room it would resemble a cactus. The heating seemed to leech every bit of moisture and goodness out of it, no matter how much we watered it or stood it in buckets of water, it always ended up dry, brown and half bald. Most of the pine needles that fell off it ended up stuck in our feet, it was like walking on a bed of (sharp) nails if you forgot to put your slippers on.

Because of this we were always encouraged to keep our distance from it. We had to give it a radius of at least a foot, avoid causing a draught, and were forbidden from slamming doors. Any sudden moves would cause it to immediately shed half a million needles, destined for the soles of our feet. Stupidly, every year, my dad hung novelty chocolates from the branches and then told us not to touch them until Christmas. Now what kid (or mother) can resist the sight of a chocolate Santa or Snowman, hanging tantalizingly just out of reach? Not us. As soon as my dad was out of the room I would put my brother on guard duty, with the promise that I would share anything I could snag, while I did my best to remove a chocolate without removing half of the pine needles.

To stand a chance of doing this I had to perch on the arm of the couch and try to lean over the thickest part of the tree without actually touching it. It took the skill of an expert contortionist to do this. We figured if we went for the ones at the back it would be less noticeable and also if I dislodged a few million needles they would fall at the back, out of sight. Usually I managed reasonably well and me and my brother shared quite a few stolen chocolates between us without ever being rumbled.

My mother wasn't quite as good at stealing as I was, she wasn't as agile and couldn't balance on the couch like me. This meant we often entered the room to find the tree wobbling with a few more bare branches then there had been ten minutes ago, and my mother trying to look innocent while at the same time trying to hide the bulging face and the chocolate dripping down her chin.

Eventually, my dad got wise to us and he would count every chocolate as he put them on the tree and then every night when he came home he would do a stocktake. I think my mother was more upset by this than we were.

For months that year I had been pestering my parents to get me a guitar for Christmas, not an electric one, just a normal one that I could strum away on. I thought it would be easy to learn and I could see myself, passing many a happy hour playing along to my records in my room. My parents said it would be just a fad and I wouldn't stick to it for five minutes before getting fed up. My mother said it would go the same way as the recorder and violin that I had taken up in junior school. I pleaded and promised that I would get a book and learn to play it properly and in the end they said they would think about it. I knew this meant that I had worn them down and that it was as good as mine.

At the beginning of December, I started snooping. My parents had recently joined a social club and as I was so grown up and responsible now (their words, not mine), I was appointed chief babysitter. I wasn't at all happy about this, I kept telling them that my brother was their baby, not mine. I hadn't asked for him so I didn't see why I should have to look after him. And also, how come every time I wanted to do something or go somewhere I wasn't considered grown up or responsible then? It was all a bit one sided in my mind. They took no notice of me whatsoever and off they went on their merry way three times a week.

At least with them out of the way I could have a good old root about for my Christmas presents. Where would they have hidden them? It was sure to be somewhere where they thought I wouldn't find them, in the loft or maybe in the back of the gas cupboard under the stairs?

They hid them in the wardrobe. Well that was crafty wasn't it, I'd never find them there would I? I shifted a box containing a 'Hot Wheels' set that my dad was pretending he'd bought for my brother but was really for him, and there it was. My guitar. They hadn't even bothered to wrap it so it was their own fault if I'd accidentally come across it wasn't it? I lifted it out and strummed it a bit, then tried to press the strings down like I'd seen people do on telly. It wasn't that easy and it hurt my fingers a bit, oh well, I'd soon get the hang of it. After a bit more investigation I discovered a couple of books about teaching yourself to play. Sorted, I'd be playing in no time.

I fiddled around for half an hour, trying to master a few chords. I had never realised playing the guitar was so difficult, maybe that's why Woody had always looked so nervous. I decided I would put it away for now and have another practice the next time my parents went out.

And so that's what I did. For the next couple of weeks, every time my parents left me to babysit I would get out the guitar and the book and give it another go. It didn't go well. The ends of my fingers were red and sore all the time, I wasn't getting any better at it and also, I found it really, really boring. By the end of three weeks I was thoroughly sick and tired of it, I never wanted to see it again as long as I lived. Unfortunately for me I still had to unwrap the bloody thing on Christmas morning and act all excited when I 'discovered' it.

Christmas morning came and there was a pile of presents under the bald tree waiting for me. There was nothing nearly as big as a guitar though. Oh, the relief. I figured maybe they couldn't afford it after all and they had taken it back to the shop, or maybe it was never mine anyway and they were hiding it for someone else. Inwardly thanking my lucky stars, I got stuck into the pile of presents - new hairdryer, Jackie annual, dodgy jumper. Then I heard my dad shout,

"Ooh what's this in the hallway, where did this come from? It's got somebody's name on it."

Oh no! I turned round to see my dad holding a big, gaudily wrapped present that was most definitely guitar shaped.

"I think it's for you."

Oh god. I had to give an Oscar winning performance as the most surprised, excited, grateful fourteen year old liar on the planet.

When I had finished gushing and thanking them and doing the whole 'Ooh you are sneaky, I thought you hadn't bought me one' job, my mother brought out the books that went with it.

"Here, have a look through these then after dinner you can play us a song, I'll join you, you play and I'll sing."

Oh, I had opened a proper can of worms here.

I took my present off to my room where I pretended to be learning to play it. After dinner, my parents and my brother all sat on the couch expecting a concert.

My mother was getting ready to start ruining the neighbours dinner and my dad had the camera out. He had already used half a roll of film taking photos of us pointing at our presents, the bald tree and the turkey and now it was my turn.

I really did try, but my fingers were so sore from the last three weeks of trying to master just one bloody chord that I couldn't get any sound out of it that wasn't horrible. Everyone sat there looking disappointed (and a bit judgmental), then my dad said,

"Well, it's not as easy as it looks, give it a couple of weeks you'll be playing a flamenco."

Then he decided we'd better put it away and break out the Quality Street, ready for The Morecambe and Wise Christmas Special.

I agreed with him and we all laughed along but I had a feeling he was in for a big disappointment.

He was. by the end of January my much longed for and pleaded for present was hanging on the wall of the second-hand shop in town. I was told in no uncertain terms never to ask for any kind of musical instrument ever again as long as I was living under their roof. My mother was really mad, when would I get it through my head that I just wasn't musical? I was dying to tell her I could ask her the same question but I figured I was in enough trouble already.

CHAPTER THIRTEEN

The Camping Trip

It was 1975 already. I had been at high school for about eighteen months now and was in my second year. At the beginning of term, we had been given a list of subjects that we had to pick from. These would be the subjects we would take our exams in and which would lead to us getting a good job. We were all called into see a Careers Officer who asked what we wanted to do when we left school and then advised us on the subjects we should be taking.

I didn't have a clue what I wanted to do when I left school, it was all I could do to get through today, never mind plan what I wanted to do two years from now.

All I knew was that it wouldn't include anything that made taking German necessary. I thought about it for a few days before the Careers Officer turned up and decided I might like to be a window dresser. I had often stood outside the windows of the big department stores in town, watching the girls that worked there dressing the mannequins and putting them in poses. It looked like fun, a bit like playing with Barbies and Sindys, but on a bigger scale.

When it was my turn to see the Careers Officer I told her of my idea. She said I would need to get a place at Art College to do that. What, just to dress up a few big dolls? I knew how to put clothes on something, I had been dressing myself for years now. I said I didn't like the sound of that but she told me I should be doing Art at "O" level just in case so I signed up for Art as one of my subjects. It was a bad idea really, I was terrible at Art. My drawings always turned out wonky and out of proportion and any sort of pottery I tried my hand at always looked like a drunk person had made it.

But I chose it anyway, much to the art teacher's delight and made a complete mess of everything I turned my hand to from then until the day I left two years later. When I left I took what was left of my masterpieces and put them in a big black bag which I deposited in the school skip on my way out.

I can't really remember what other subjects I chose, after the first year everything just merged into one big boring lesson. I couldn't wait to get away. The only lesson I ever liked was English, maybe because it was the only thing I was ever any good at. I quite liked history as well, when we had a good teacher although didn't happen very often.

Around March of that year a form went around the girls in our year asking if any of us would be interested in a week of camping up near Scarborough. It was to be set up for the end of June and a few of us from my class jumped at the chance. A week off school, topping up our tans with the chance to sneak off into Scarborough to go shopping and play in the amusements. Who wouldn't want to go.

Melanie didn't. She said it wouldn't be all fun, school trips never were, but I dismissed her words and signed up. I was thinking how sorry she'd be that she missed it when I came home with all my tales of the good time we'd had.

The next few weeks I went around scrounging pots and pans and camping stuff that I would need, Malcom lent me his sleeping bag that he hadn't used since he was in the scouts. I turned it inside out and left it outside for a week before spraying it all over with some Just Musk that I had been bought for Christmas.

It seemed no time at all before the big day dawned. We were setting off on Monday morning and coming back Friday night so it wasn't exactly a full week but it was still five full days with no school. The teacher in charge of the trip was Mrs Miller the adulteress, although actually the affair between her and Mr Grayson was over now, it had been finished for some time. We all knew this because for the last six months he had been following her around the school like a love sick puppy pleading for another chance. He often popped up in the middle of a P.E lesson with a bunch of flowers and a hopeful expression on his face. Mrs Miller would sigh loudly, drag him over to the doorway and whisper very discreetly;

"GET IT THROUGH YOUR HEAD JOHN, IT'S OVER."

Before stomping back in and throwing a basketball at someone's head. There was no need to take it out on us just because she couldn't control her love life.

When Mr Grayson wasn't around she was an ok teacher and if it had to be a P.E teacher who was coming with us we would rather it was her than Miss Hymer. We wouldn't have felt safe in our tents with her prowling around the campsite in the middle of the night, looking for a pulled hamstring to massage.

So, as I said, the great day dawned and we all met up at school at half past nine, backpacks heaving with all the stuff we needed for five days and nights in the wilderness. Most of us had also packed make up, going out clothes and some not so sensible shoes for whenever the chance came to escape off to Scarborough. We boarded the minibus and headed off for our mini break in the sun.

I don't really know what we were expecting but it wasn't what we discovered when we arrived. Our camp site was in the middle of a massive forest, all you could see wherever you looked were trees. For the last half hour on the bus we wound through tiny little lanes no bigger than dirt tracks and the further we went, the higher we seemed to go. I swear our ears were popping.

When the bus finally arrived at the entrance to a field we were getting worried. We had pictured a nice little camping area a little way from the beach and the bright lights of the amusement arcades and the fairground. Instead of this, we were miles away from civilization, I had never been so far away from other people.

Mrs Miller got us organized into groups and we started unloading our tents from the coach. The school had provided the tents from somewhere, they were massive, the one I was in slept around six of us but there was still plenty of room so long as you didn't want to stand up. The only tent I had ever put up was made from my mother's clothes horse and a few bedsheets. Me and Melanie had 'camped' out a few times in my back garden in the summer when we were a bit younger.

I can't remember quite how long it took us to get the tents up but it was getting dark before we finished. Mrs Miller had got the camp fire going and we were trying to figure out how to cook sausages without a cooker. A couple of other women teachers had come along to chaperone us. One of them was Mrs Pearson, the maths teacher and I didn't know the other one.

After we had finished eating our supper we were told to use the toilet and then get to bed, apparently we had a big day tomorrow. The toilet turned out to be a chemical one, housed in something that felt like a cupboard. There was to be a rota whereby every day two people were responsible for carrying it away and emptying it. This was horrifying news, none of us had even thought about toilet facilities. We got into our pyjamas while trying to digest this new piece of information, this little holiday didn't seem to be such a good idea now.

We were just getting our sleeping bags organized when the tent flap opened and Mrs Pearson came crawling in.

"Can I bunk with you girls?" she trilled "It's a bit cramped in our tent until we get all the unpacking done tomorrow."

Before we could answer she started undressing.

"All girls together isn't it?" she laughed.

We sat in stunned silence as she pulled her top over her head, releasing two massive bouncy bosoms loose into the tent. None of us knew where to look. I suddenly found Gillian, who was next to me, utterly fascinating. I couldn't take my eyes off the two pink sponge rollers that she had put in her fringe.

She, in turn was equally fascinated with the zip on her sleeping bag. Everyone was looking intently at something, anything as long as it wasn't the two new bouncy visitors to our tent. What was wrong with this woman, was she another Miss Hymer? Thankfully, she put her nightie on and we could all look up again.

Finally, we got settled into our sleeping bags. I went to sleep that night thinking of ways to avoid going to the toilet for the next five days. I didn't want another nasty surprise. Clearly, this woman had no boundaries.

The next day we were up bright and early, well early. None of us had slept much, every little noise had us sitting up clutching our sleeping bags in terror, there were owls hooting and animals snuffling about in the bushes nearby. Added to that was the noise of the warthog in the sleeping bag next to mine Apparently once Gillian did get to sleep she snored like a wounded pig, a fact which she strongly denied when we informed her of it the next morning.

We went outside to see who was on breakfast duty. None of us were that hungry really due to the fact we had each packed half a sweet shop in our backpacks. Luckily, that morning I had avoided the toilet emptying. Instead, me and another girl had the task of hiking fifty miles to the nearest farm to bring back a big pail of water. Well it felt like fifty miles. By the time we got back we were hot, sweaty and exhausted, plus we had spilled half the water and drunk a lot of it as well. It was boiling hot that summer and was already hot by eight in the morning.

I was looking forward to a morning spent lounging around the campsite, maybe drawing wildflowers or studying leaves. Not to be. We were each given a map, a list of things we had to collect from the wild and without any advice on which berries were poisonous or anything, we were sent off into the forest. Mrs

Miller said it should take us about an hour to complete the trail.

We set off, deeply regretting that we had ever become involved with this trip. Clearly we had been duped, we were obviously on a Duke of Edinburgh Award Scheme. Either that or the Careers Officer had signed us all up for the army and this was our training course. If so, we were all about to fail miserably, within ten minutes of setting off we were hopelessly lost. None of us could make sense of our maps, we weren't even sure which way up we should be holding them. I just wanted to go home, Blue Peter never prepared me for this.

After what seemed like four or five hours and with half the group in tears now, we heard someone coming. Thank god, they'd come looking for us. No they hadn't. Into view came about forty girl scouts, marching along with backpacks and holding little bags full of pine cones and leaves and stuff. They were obviously on the same scavenger hunt as we were, difference being, they knew what they were doing. We asked them the way out of the forest so they asked where we were staying but none of us knew. In the end they told us to follow them back to where they were camped. Maybe someone there could find out who we belonged to.

We followed them for a bit. We had all given up on looking for the things on our lists, survival was more important. After a while we caught a glimpse of something orange through the trees, it was our tents, we had found our way back. We came staggering out of the forest like a little gang of escaped hostages, almost weeping with relief. We were   expecting the teachers to be frantic with worry about us. Instead they were stretched out on blankets, dressed in bikinis, sunbathing. Unbelievable, these were supposed to be the responsible adults who were looking after us. They must have had the same thought as us, a week off school, lounging around in the sun. We were being used here.

For the rest of that day we did nothing, we were too tired from all the hiking. At least the exhaustion meant we slept better that night. Also, Chesty Morgan had gone back to her own tent so we were spared the embarrassment of the strip show.

The next day was even hotter, it was unbearable. We were sent off on the same hike again, with the same maps and the same lists, this time the teachers came with us. I should think so. We didn't find half the things we were looking for but at least we didn't get so lost this time. We came back half mad with dehydration and had a bit of free time before supper but there was nothing to do. The bright lights of Scarborough seemed as far away to us as London.

That night we were awakened by someone walking around the tents. We all sat up, terrified again. What if it was some homicidal maniac with an axe? Gillian said it must be someone going to the toilet but we never heard the door opening and it was right near our tent. We kept listening and there was definitely someone out there. Then we heard a man's voice, whispering,

"Sharon, Sharon, are you in there".

We heard more movement from one of the other tents, then Mrs Miller hissing,

"Get in here you bloody idiot before you wake them all up."

That was enough, we all stuck our heads out of the tent flap to see what was going on. In the darkness, we could make out Mrs Miller and the figure of a man, they were arguing.

Then the penny dropped, it was Mr Grayson. He had followed Mrs Miller here for another chance to rekindle their romance. Ooh this was good, how was she going to explain his presence in the morning? This trip was turning out to be interesting after all.

The next morning, we all staggered out of the tent exhausted again. We had stayed awake half the night speculating on what was going on across the field in Mrs Miller's tent. She was sharing with the two other teachers so god knows what they must have thought to their midnight visitor.

The breakfast bench was set up with boxes of cereal waiting for us. Mrs Miller was fiddling around with something or other while the other two ladies were eating in silence. Sitting at the end of the table with a look of shame on his face was Mr Grayson. Mrs Miller looked up at us all.

"Look who's dropped by girls" she announced, trying to look all bright and breezy. "Mr Grayson was on his way back from up north, he thought he'd call and see us. He's on his way home shortly aren't you Mr Grayson?"

She knew that we all knew what was really going on.

Mr Grayson, meanwhile was looking like he might throw up, I think he was regretting his grand gesture now. We sat down and all ate our cornflakes in silence, wondering what might happen next.

After breakfast we were supposed to be going on another nature walk but it was getting hotter by the minute. We were all bright red from being out in the sun for the last couple of days and some of us (including me) had headaches. It was decided that we would stay around the campsite that day and try and keep cool. Two of the girls were sent off to bring back the water and we were told to drink plenty that day.

As the day wore on it got hotter and hotter, I began to feel sick. In the end, to get out of the sun we went for a walk through the forest with Mrs Pearson, it was cooler in the forest. When we returned Mr Grayson was laid out on a blanket looking decidedly sick. He was telling Mrs Miller there was no way he could leave, he was too ill. We could tell she didn't believe him and thought he was trying to pull a fast one.

All that day he lay down swearing he felt awful. By now we all had a bit of heatstroke but we weren't complaining as much as him. When bedtime came there was much hissing and whispering between him and Mrs Miller. She wanted him out of there but he was insisting he was too ill.

In the end he stayed the night again. Mrs Pearson took her bosoms to bunk in another tent and he stayed with Mrs Miller in hers. In the middle of the night we were woken again, this time by the sound of engines, we could see flashing lights through the canvas.

Poking our heads out of the tent again we were just in time to see Mr Grayson, strapped to a stretcher, being loaded into the back of an ambulance. Dear god, had Mrs Miller tried to kill him? Some school trip this was turning out to be.

It turned out Mr Grayson wasn't scamming, he had really bad appendicitis, and his appendix was on the verge of bursting. Someone had driven to the farm nearby to use their phone and call for help and now he was being carted off to hospital.

We went back to our tents and tried to sleep again, I don't think I had ever gone without sleep as much as I had since we arrived in this bloody field. I much preferred camping in my back garden, even if it was underneath a clothes horse.

The next morning, Mrs Pearson was going home in her car, she couldn't stay as long as the other teachers. Before she went she asked if anyone wanted to go back early as she could drop them off at their homes. This was my chance, I had my bag packed and one leg in the car before she could finish speaking. The others all wanted to stay, they said Mrs Miller had said they could go to Scarborough the next day but I didn't believe a word of it. I wanted my own bed. My head was throbbing fit to burst and I felt awful. I just wanted out of the sun.

I bid farewell to the rest of the happy campers and I was off. I would rather be trapped in a car with Mrs Pearson and her bazookas for two hours than spend another second in this place. If she had driven home topless I still wouldn't have cared as long as she got me out of there.

A couple of hours later and I was being deposited on the doorstep at home. All I wanted to do was go and lay down in my nice cool, soothing bedroom. My mother greeted me at the door with;

"We paid for the week you know."

Before telling me that there was a surprise waiting for me upstairs. Oh what fresh hell was this, my parent's surprises weren't usually good ones.

I went upstairs with a sinking feeling in my (already upset) stomach, I opened the door and it hit me. My dad had decorated my bedroom for me while I had been away. All my posters had been removed and the walls were now covered in bright orange and white triangular wallpaper. To top it all off my mother had 'accessorized' with a bright orange quilted bedspread and orange flowered lampshades. My already aching head felt like someone had just stuck a red hot poker through the back of it. I instinctively shut my eyes to protect my poor brain while I delved into my backpack to retrieve my sunglasses. Melanie had been right; school trips were never as good as you thought they were going to be.

CHAPTER FOURTEEN

Should They Bleed That Much?

After the camping fiasco, we were only back at school for another month before it was time for the six weeks' holidays again. For the final few weeks Mrs Miller was very quiet and Mr Grayson didn't put in an appearance as he was still recuperating from his surgery. Incidentally, the others never did get to go into Scarborough just I predicted. They hung around the campsite getting more burnt and dehydrated until it was time to go home. I don't think any of us signed up for any school trips again as long as we were there

That was the summer I was determined to finally get my ears pierced. All my friends had theirs done by now (except Melanie whose parents were even more old fashioned than mine) I had been nagging my parents for the last two years with no luck. My dad would just tell me to wait until I was older, and anyway, if I was meant to have holes in my ears I would have been born with them. Meanwhile my mother would fall back on her old favourite, only prostitutes had pierced ears.

The list of things that only prostitutes had was growing steadily longer, anything I mentioned was met with the same reply. Only prostitutes had ankle strap shoes, ankle bracelets, pierced earrings, tattoos, and bizarrely, red handbags and red lipstick, in fact, most things red were suspect. I don't know how my mother knew so much about prostitution but she seemed to be quite the expert. By now I knew what a prostitute was but by my mother's strange ideas it looked as though half the women in our area were supplementing their income in this way. Not for the first time (or the second), I came to the conclusion that my mother was a nut job.

About two weeks into the holidays one of my friends who still had virgin earlobes Vicky, was finally given the go ahead from her parents to get pierced. Green with envy I went with her to get them done. We caught the bus into town and found the place we were looking for, it was a caravan parked in the car park of a big supermarket. There was a board outside advertising ear piercing with pictures of different sparkly studs. We went inside not knowing what to expect. The last time we had been in a caravan was the year before at the fair, getting our fortunes told. Mine had been crap, just as I had been expecting, I think Gypsy Rose Lee had met my mother.

Inside the caravan it was really clean and clinical, more like a hospital than anything else. It smelt like surgical spirit and the lady doing the piercing had a white coat on, we were impressed. Vicky paid her money and sat in the black leather chair. She picked the 9-carat gold plain studs and the woman loaded one up in a sort of a gun. She drew two dots on Vicky's earlobes for targets and put the gun to the first one, I was waiting with bated breath. There was a loud click and it was done. Vicky jumped a bit for a second but it was over and she said it didn't hurt. The woman shot her other ear and that was it, it was over, she produced a mirror and let Vicky have a look at her shiny new ears and then we left. I was beside myself with jealousy, all the way home I was cursing my parents for being so old fashioned and stuck in their ways.

Back home I told them how clinical and sterilised everything had been, and how small and understated Vicky's studs were. I tried to convince them that I would never want to wear anything bigger than that in my ears and that there would never, ever be anything dangly hanging from my earlobes. I promised and promised that I would never be mistaken for a prostitute.

After about four hours of this I finally wore them down. They agreed that as long as I went to the same place and got the same small studs as Vicky I could get it done. My mother said that if I came home with studs any bigger than I had described she would take them out herself and throw them in the bin and that would be that. I had done it, I had finally convinced them. I think deep down, my dad had just become so uncomfortable with me saying the word 'prostitute' over and over, that he would have agreed to anything just to get me out of the room.

I had to wait until the next Saturday to get my new ears, Vicky came with me and together we caught the bus into town again. This time, when we came to the car park there was no sign of the caravan or the board, it was gone. I was distraught. It had taken me all this time to convince my parents to let me do this, I might never get another chance. If I went home unpierced they might change their minds again. Then Vicky said she knew of a little shop where you could get it done but it was quite a walk from town. I didn't care how far I had to walk (I had plenty of walking experience growing up with my parents), so off we went.

Half an hour later we were at the shop. It was a little grubby place that sold cheap costume jewellery and naff ornaments of animals wearing clothes, the sort my mother loved. We went inside and I asked the girl behind the counter about getting my ears done, she sent us into a back room. It looked like my Nanna's living room when I was little, there was a big old lady sitting on a faded armchair watching telly. The girl shouted that I had come for my ears piercing and the old lady asked me for my money. I was a bit dubious, this was nothing like the clinical environment that Vicky had been pierced in.

The old woman told me to sit in her armchair, then she produced a metal thing that looked nothing like the other woman had used on Vicky. Instead of a small stud she brought out a pair of little gold hoops called sleepers. They were really small but they weren't studs, what would my mother think to these. Well I was here now and I had paid my money so I sat down.

The woman clamped the thing to one of my earlobes and before I had time to tell her she hadn't marked my ears she crunched it closed on my earlobe. It was agony, I felt and heard something crunch as the pain shot through my ear. While I was still reeling from the pain and the shock she attacked my other ear, this one hurt even more.

She wiped my ears with a tissue, told me to rotate them every day, then asked for her chair back. That was it, we were dismissed. We walked back outside without another word, my ears were throbbing with pain. I asked Vicky if hers had felt like that but she said no, she hadn't really felt anything. We started walking back into town. After a couple of minutes I saw Vicky's alarmed face and realised I could feel something trickling down my neck. I was bleeding from both new earholes. I wiped the blood away with the tissue from the shop and waited for it to stop. It didn't. All the way back into town I was mopping up blood and there was no sign of it slowing down. I began to feel quite alarmed, could a person bleed to death from having their ears pierced?

When we reached the town centre we went into the ladies toilets to inspect the damage. My ears looked awful, the lobes were swollen and bright red. Even after we washed the blood off they were still really red, how could I go home like this? My mother would have a duck fit. I soaked some paper towels in cold water and sat down with them pressed to my ears for a bit to try and stop the bleeding.

Eventually, it slowed down and began to scab but my ears were still throbbing with pain. I couldn't stay out forever though so we headed for the bus stop and home. By the time I got off the bus the bleeding had stopped completely and I just had two lovely scabby ears. Arriving home, I tried to sneak in quietly to avoid attention but my parents were in the kitchen when I opened the door.

"Let's have a look then." said my mother, pulling my hair back out of the way.

She took one look and gasped, "Oh my god, look at this, look what she's done to herself." My dad joined her in peering at my poor defiled earlobes. I tried to explain that the lovely sterilised caravan lady had run out of studs and had given me these sleepers instead, but that they were just as safe and very small. When they asked about the redness and the scabs I told them the very clean, professional lady had said that sometimes this happens if you have very sensitive ears but it was nothing to worry about. I was making all of this up as I went along.

My mother was horrified and told me to take them out immediately, luckily my dad stepped in and said it would probably make it worse if I fiddled with them any more. He told me to bathe them in salt water and wait until they settled down. Phew, I was saved.

They did settle down over the next few days and because my mother had got used to seeing them by then, she relented and let me keep them in. I had to wait six weeks before I could take them out and put new earrings in as they had to heal properly. I had already bought some nice new sparkly studs to wear when the others came out. When that day finally came I realised just what a hatchet job that woman had done on me. The left ear was fine but the right one was completely odd. The hole at the front of my ear was about a quarter of an inch lower than the hole at the back, they didn't match up at all. It took ages to get the right stud in and by the time I finished my ear was as sore as the day I had it done.

To this day, every time I stand fiddling around trying to get my earring in that ear I curse the day I ever went into the back of that grubby shop.

And I still feel slightly wicked wearing my dangly earrings, especially as I've got a tattoo and red handbag as well.

CHAPTER FIFTEEN

The Big Freeze

1975 was the year my parents bought a freezer. Before they bought it we had to make do with the tiny ice box in the top of the fridge. All you could really fit in it was a bag of frozen peas and our ice lollies so when the new freezer came my parents went a bit mental.

Overnight they became obsessed with freezing things. They went out and bought hundreds of freezer bags in all different sizes and began to plan what they were going to freeze. According to my dad we were going to save a fortune on food because we could buy everything in bulk and freeze it. It became like a military operation, lists were drawn up, measurements were taken and out came the bags on wheels.

As we were still without a car, a fact that would never change until me and brother grew up and got our own cars, the bag on wheels was my mother's only way of getting the weekly shop home. She had bought the extra large one but we also had a smaller one so that on really big shopping days me and my mother could pull one each. I hated doing this in case my friends saw me pulling it along like a little old lady and took the mickey out of me. I would trundle along behind my mother cursing my dad for not driving. He had never even had a driving lesson never mind take his test but he insisted that he could drive if he needed to. This was because when he was eighteen and in the army he had once moved a lorry across a car park.

Every Saturday when it was time for the 'big' shop we would all walk to the village a couple of miles away. We had a supermarket on our estate but my parents thought it wasn't upmarket enough and you got a better class of people at the village one. For people from a council estate they were such snobs. So off we would go tramping up the country lane, past the gypsy camp, dragging our bags behind us, it took about half an hour to walk there. The only good bit was about half way there, we had to pass a field with a horse in it.

Over the weeks, I had become friends with the horse and I used to take it an apple or bits of carrot every week. It always came to the gate to wait when it saw us coming. One afternoon, my mother decided to make friends with it as well and came over to stroke it. I don't know what she did to it but it let out the most enormous sneeze and blew half a gallon of horsey snot all over my mother's new powder blue jacket. She went nuts, I thought for one awful minute she was going to punch my nice new friend straight in the muzzle. My dad did his best to mop her up with tissues but she still had to go into the posh village with snotty stains all over her. I daren't laugh at the time but the next week I gave the horse a longer stroke and an extra apple.

Anyway, with the list of frozen items in my dad's pocket we set off for the supermarket. When we got there I sat outside reading my Jackie magazine and left them to it. The only thing I was ever needed for was to help in pulling the shopping home. No one but my dad was ever allowed to put the shopping into the bags. He did it with military precision, it was like something off the Krypton Factor the way he could get everything in with the boxes and tins all arranged so that every inch of space was used to its full advantage. It was quite an art. I don't know if he had picked this up in the army as well, maybe that's how they had to fill their backpacks.

When they came out again the two bags on wheels were full to bursting and they also had about half a dozen shopping bags as well. I was beginning to think the new freezer wouldn't be big enough. We set off for home, me and my mother taking turns to pull one bag on wheels while my dad pulled the other one, we all had shopping bags as well. Even my brother had to carry a bag and he never usually had to help.

When we reached home I left them to it and went out to Vicky's. When I left they were unloading the bags, all excited and looking forward to filling the freezer. I thought they were easily entertained.

My mother felt dead posh to have a freezer. My Aunty Dolly had bought one a couple of years ago and my mother had been green with envy. She was always like that whenever Aunty Dolly got something new, she wouldn't rest until she had the same thing. Some people try to keep up with the Jones', my mother tried to keep up with Aunty Dolly.

When I returned a couple of hours later I was met by a sight. The kitchen was full of pork chops, it looked like they bought a full pig's worth. They had taken all of these chops out of the big bag and they were bagging them individually in little freezer bags. Before they fastened the bags they had little straws and they were sucking all the air out of each bag before sealing it. It looked bizarre. They tried to get me to join in but I didn't want to be sucking the taste of cold, dead pig into my mouth so I politely declined.

It took them half the day to get everything unpacked and resealed ready for freezing. They repeated the pork chop saga with pieces of chicken, half a million sausages, fish fingers, peas and god knows how many frozen vegetables. My mother was so proud. For the next few weeks she never shut up going on about it to anyone who would listen. She would tell the neighbours;

"I don't know what we're going to have for tea, I'll have to look in the freezer."

It didn't matter whether it came out of the freezer or not, it was still the same old crap.

My mother had felt just as posh a couple of years earlier when we had finally had a telephone 'put in'. She felt like a proper lady of the manor now, she would go around asking people if they were on the phone just so she could tell them that she was. As soon as it was in and the telephone engineer had gone she started developing her 'telephone voice'. It was hysterical, she sounded like the Queen. Me and my dad would listen at the door when she was on the phone weeing ourselves laughing. My dad would tell her to stop talking like that but she would just say she wasn't doing anything, she'd always had a nice speaking voice. As far as that went her 'speaking' was on a par with her 'singing'.

My Aunty Dolly would ring our house and my mother would answer in her Royal voice. Aunty Dolly would say;

"What are you talking like that for you silly sod, talk properly."

This would annoy my mother no end. Mind you, Aunty Dolly's telephone voice was even funnier. She would add a 'H' on to the front of all her words when they shouldn't be there. She used to run a catalogue and she would ring them up to order things giving her account number. She had a lot of '0's in her number and we would all have to stifle our giggles when she was announcing;

"Two, Three, Seven, Double Ho, Double Ho, Four, Ho." It never got any less funny over the years.

I was always in trouble for being on the phone. My dad would stand over me pointing to his watch whenever I was talking to anyone. He would say;

"You've been at school with them all day, what can you possibly have to talk about?" He never understood that some things couldn't be discussed at school between lessons and had to be talked about at length later on. Things of great importance like;

"Did you see the state of Debbie's hair this morning" and "Where do you think that girl in Mrs Waller's class got them shoes?"

See? Things of great importance.

The great filling of the freezer carried on for a good few years. Every time it started to look a bit empty, out would come the wheelie bags and off we would go again. Apart from the supermarket shopping I always tried to avoid going anywhere with my family.

Sometimes my dad would insist that we all go somewhere together and I would be forced to tag along. My dad would always find somewhere that we could sit down and have a meal together. I hated this, it always ended in trouble. My brother still only ate beans but my dad would try desperately to get him to try other things. He would refuse point blank and my dad would get furious with him without actually raising his voice in case people looked at us. He would be hissing in whispers and nodding his head a lot while my brother sat there, arms folded and lips clamped tight together refusing to try anything that wasn't beans.

Meanwhile, my mother always found something to complain about. I remember one cafe we were in once where she kept insisting that her peas were cold. My dad told her to eat them faster then but she wouldn't let it drop, she was going to complain. My dad was doing his 'I'm furious but you'd never know it by looking at me' face and telling her,

"Don't you dare say anything, it doesn't matter, just eat the bloody things."

She sulked a bit but started eating them. After a few minutes the waitress brought us more tea and asked if everything was alright. We all looked at my mother, she was dying to say something but I think my dad might have been kicking her under the table.

"Everything was very nice thank you." My dad replied.

Still nothing from my mother, she was going to keep quiet for once. Just as the waitress was turning away she could contain herself no longer.

"My peas were cold" she called out to her.

I held my breath, my dad's face was a picture.

"No, they weren't, she just took a long time to eat them." He said with a nervous laugh. This annoyed my mother who started telling him she knew cold peas when she was served them.

This was my dad's worst nightmare, she was causing a scene. The waitress said she'd bring the manager to deal with it. Deal with what, was he going to go boil some more peas? We had all finished eating now. My dad's face was purple now, people at the other tables were starting to look at us. Out came the manager to see what the problem was. My mother told him the same thing;

"My peas were cold."

He was very sympathetic to her plight, he offered to get her some more but she said she wasn't hungry as she'd already eaten the cold ones. He said he would knock the price of the peas off the bill but my dad wasn't having that. He could afford to pay for peas, hot or cold and he wasn't taking charity from anyone.

In the end, he almost dragged my mother out of the cafe. He was fuming with her but nobody would have known, all the way home they argued in hisses and whispers while keeping normal polite faces on. I never actually saw them have a proper row. I walked about ten paces behind them trying to pretend I'd never met them. My brother said it wouldn't have happened if we'd all asked for beans.

CHAPTER SIXTEEN

Who Ate All The Pies

Christmas came and went again. After the New Year had been seen in, our bald, dry tree was put out for the dustmen and we all got ready to see what 1976 would bring. I was fifteen now and I had come to accept by now that I wasn't adopted and that I really did belong in this family. It had taken a long time to come to terms with.

At school, we had all moved up a year again, we only had one more year left before we were all to be let loose on the world. I wasn't thinking about that yet though, at the moment I couldn't see past the next Saturday and what I could buy in town with my pocket money. I was starting to go out more on my own all the time now. On a Saturday, some of us would all go into town for the day and spend our time buying bits of rubbish that we could afford while gazing longingly at the things we couldn't. At dinner time we would go into the market for lunch, this was a very posh event. We would go into a red and white stripey tent where the floor was covered in sawdust. Then we'd go to the counter and order patty and chips with a coke then spend half an hour sitting on ripped plastic stools on the sawdust floor, eating our meal with a wooden fork. It was the height of sophistication.

On a Thursday night we would all meet up at the under eighteens disco. This was held in the large hall behind the Blind Institute, and actually belonged to the Institute. We all just used to say we were going to the disco at Blind Institute. My mother took this as an opportunity to brag about me to the neighbours. She was always looking for things about her children to brag about, unfortunately, we never did anything bragworthy. On this occasion she did her usual trick of reinventing her life to better suit what she thought it should be and she told all the neighbours I was doing charity work. She told them I was teaching blind people to dance.

Can you imagine? Me at fifteen years old trying to show people who couldn't see how to do 'The Bump'. I really don't know where she got these ideas from. My dad was just as bad though. Every week when I set off he would shout after me;

"Don't forget your white stick."

I was still friends with Melanie but now that we were in different classes for different subjects we had both started making other friends as well. Sometimes we all met up with both sets of friends but more often now we were going different ways. I was spending most of my time with Vicky now, she lived about fifteen minutes away from my house. Every time we went clothes shopping we bought exactly the same things. We had matching jeans or skirts, the same tops and shoes, we even had the same haircuts. When we saw a leather jacket we both liked, we saved up until we had enough money and then we both bought one. We must have looked like Tweedle Dee and Tweedle Dum.

When really big platform shoes came in, we were both in the queue to buy a pair. Mine were orange with big studs all the way around them and they had eight inch heels and six inch platforms. I loved them but my dad said I looked like Frankenstein's monster in them. I would just laugh at him then look down and pat him on the head on my way out.

One day me and Vicky decided to go to the cinema to see 'The Omen'. We weren't old enough as you had to be eighteen but it was easy to get in to see films back then. To get to the cinema doors there was a big flight of stairs, the cinema had once been a big grand place. This proved quite difficult for us as we were both wearing our platforms. We had to hold each other up like a pair of old ladies as we navigated our way up the stairs very slowly, one step at a time. We were exhausted when we got there and were glad of a sit down. By the time I got home my feet would be killing me but I would never admit that to my parents.

Sometimes we would give the Blind Institute a miss and go into town to the under eighteens disco. This was held in a proper nightclub, once a week they would open the place up just to kids and serve nothing but crisps and soft drinks. We weren't satisfied with this. About five of us would meet up and then we would all chip in a few pence to buy a bottle of cider. Then we'd walk the rest of the way into town drinking cider from the bottle and trying to convince ourselves that we were drunk.

We weren't, we weren't even tipsy but we acted as if we'd had ten pints, it was embarrassing. We used to leave our biggest platform shoes at home on these nights as they were hard enough to walk in never mind dance. Anyway, nobody should ever be drunk in charge of a pair of platforms that big. It could end in a trip to A&E!

That year at school we had to attend sex education lessons and we were dreading it. I've heard a lot of schools separate the girls and boys for these lessons to lessen the embarrassment. Not ours, we all had to sit together, it was excruciating. The boys giggled and cracked jokes while the girls sat rigid in our seats, faces glowing bright pink. Mrs Seymour, who was taking the lessons tried to lighten the mood by throwing condoms at us all but it didn't work. I sat there wondering how I was going to bring this up at the tea table tonight when my dad asked what I'd been doing today.

One girl in our class should probably have attended these lessons a bit sooner. She was only in one class with me so I didn't really know her. Her friends were in different classes too, she was nice enough but a bit quiet. That year she started to put a bit of weight on, after a few more weeks she was looking decidedly podgy. When the podge grew steadily bigger we all took notice and realised maybe it wasn't because she'd been eating too many pies. A few more weeks went by and by now the teachers were starting to notice as well. One brave girl in our class plucked up the courage to broach the subject and asked her delicately if she thought she might be 'up the duff'. This was met by a polite,

"Of course not, I've just got a bit fatter".

We didn't know if she was trying to throw us off the scent or if she really was in denial. Some of us were still a bit dim in that area but we knew enough to know a pregnant belly when we saw one. By the time she could no longer fit properly behind her desk, the teachers started to look seriously worried every time they had to take the lesson. Sometimes we could see her jump slightly and it was obvious that the baby was kicking her. The teachers were so on edge by now they could hardly stop looking at her, I think they were terrified that her waters would break and they'd be forced to deliver a baby in the middle of the lesson. Still, if anyone said anything to her about it she'd smile sweetly and tell them not to be daft.

Eventually I think the teachers did something about it and she disappeared from our lessons for a while. She came back before we all left for good, looking a lot slimmer but smelling of baby sick. When we asked how she was we discovered the pies had turned out to be a baby boy. She seemed a lot more surprised than we were bless her.

Even though we were all between fifteen and sixteen years old it was quite surprising how many girls were actually going out with the male teachers. Today it would be a scandal, the teacher would be dragged into court and sent to prison and the girl would make a few bob selling her story to the newspapers. Back then nobody took much notice, the only thing that annoyed us was the favouritism. We all knew that one girl was dating the maths teacher, he was in his thirties and married but we didn't care about that. The only thing that bothered us was the fact that she always came top of the class when we all knew she could hardly add up two and two.

One of our history teachers took a bit of a fancy to Vicky. She was horrified by this. I would tell her that at least he was only in his twenties and single but she wasn't amused. He would make excuses to get her to stay behind after class and she would threaten to kill me if I left her alone with him. So I would sit there like a gooseberry, swinging my legs, perched on a desk waiting while he tried to find some reason to get rid of me. Sometimes he asked me to wait outside for her so I would stand outside the door with my nose pressed up against the glass window in the door watching them. Eventually I think he realised that three was a crowd and he moved on to another girl in the class. She ended up marrying him so that was a happy ending for everyone. Vicky escaped his pervy clutches and the other girl got a husband who could tell her everything about the Magna Carta and the French Revolution.

CHAPTER SEVENTEEN

Hi de Hi

The summer of 1976 was the hottest, driest summer that Britain had ever seen. There had been no rain for ages and all the reservoirs were really low on water.

The ground was dry and cracked everywhere and there was a hosepipe ban in every part of the country. Every day for weeks and weeks the temperature was in the eighties and nineties and it would be unbearably hot even first thing in the morning. It was the hottest year since records began, a few hundred years ago.

The government put in special measures, standpipes were being installed all over Yorkshire ready for when we could no longer use our taps. They put messages on the telly and radio asking everyone to think before turning on a tap. We were told to use washing up water to flush our toilets and asked to bathe in no more than five inches of water. All the adults talked of nothing else, it was like the blackouts all over again, the newspapers were full of it every day.

In our house my dad was having a fit. His garden was his pride and joy and it was killing him to see it all drying up and withering away before his eyes. His lovely green grass was reduced to a pile of dried up straw, his flowers were wilting and drying up and his vegetables were beyond saving.

He wouldn't give up without a fight though. The washing up water that was supposed to be used for flushing the toilet was syphoned off into his watering can used to try and save his garden. When we were having a bath in our five inches of water he was standing outside, bucket at the ready shouting;

"Don't you dare pull that bloody plug."

He even went so far as trying to beg the neighbours for their washing up water as well. Bless him, however much he tried it was never enough and his garden withered away into a brown, cracked wilderness.

All the grownups hated it but we loved it, it was the best summer ever. We had finished school for the six weeks' holidays and there was nothing to do but lay in the sun, eating ice lollies. Every day I would get into my bikini and drag the sun lounger out. My dad would be out topless, still trying to save his garden while we got browner and browner.

My dad still insisted that we use sun protection so he would break out his trusted bottle of olive oil and vinegar and insist we all applied it at regular intervals. Once again we all lay sizzling in our oil while the neighbours would get sudden cravings for fish and chips. I think our family did the chip shop up the street a favour that summer. One whiff of our family over the fence and they were all queuing up outside the shop.

Sometimes I would drag myself off the deck chair to go out with my friends, we would attempt to go do something fun but it was always so hot that we would wilt from the heat and usually end up laid out in someones garden or in the park. A few times we went to the outdoor swimming pool but as everyone had the same idea all we could do was bob around with everyone else all packed in like sardines.

That year my dad booked for us all to go for a week's holiday at Butlins. I was allowed to take a friend with me. Vicky was going somewhere with her family and Melanie was otherwise engaged so I took one of my other friends, Tina. We were dead excited to be going and spent ages discussing what we were going to pack, not that either of us had that much anyway. We set off on the coach on a Saturday morning in late August, it was still hot but a bit cooler than it had been. Me and Tina had our Jackie summer specials to read on the way and my brother had his comics.

When we arrived, we had to board a little train with carriages along with all the other families and their luggage. At various spots along the way people would get dropped off at their chalet. We were the last people left on the train, our chalet was at the very end of the camp. When we got inside ours we were quite impressed (remember we didn't get around much). We had two bedrooms, a bathroom and a little kitchen with a cooker. Me and Tina had one room with twin beds in it and my parents and brother had the family room. Before we even thought about unpacking anything, me and Tina were off to have a look around.

There were kids our age everywhere. There was a fair with rides that were free to anyone staying at the camp so we jumped straight onto the waltzers. By the time we went home a week later we had bruises on both our bums from being thrown around on the rides all week.

In one of the cafes we discovered that all the kids met up there every day, there were no adults anywhere, they all went to different cafes. We found ourselves adopted by a gang of Scottish kids, girls and boys, all our age and for the rest of the week we went around with them. After a few days we acquired some kids from West Yorkshire as well so we had quite the little gang.

My parents hardly saw us that week. We spent all our time with our new friends, we bought Kiss Me Quick hats and squashed ourselves into photo booths for dozens of photos showing bits of someone's ear and the odd nose or two. We would be out all day then we would come back to the chalet to get changed and get ready for the nightly disco in one of the kids clubs.

My parents would get ready to go to their club, taking my brother with them. On the way, we would stop off at the beer garden and my dad said as we were almost sixteen we were allowed half of lager. Just the one mind, while my parents were with us. Then they would wave us off to the disco while they went their own way. What they didn't know was that when they were out of sight we sloped off to the bar for a few halves of lager before we went to the disco. It was so easy to get served there, we just said it was for my dad who was sitting 'over there'. Then we waved in the general direction of anyone, and, because it was such a friendly place, someone would always wave back.

Sorted.

My parents were having a ball as well. There was always something going on, the place was full of Redcoats, people in red blazers who worked there providing entertainment. There were contests and competitions everywhere. You couldn't walk more than a few steps without someone trying to drag you off to a knobbly knees parade or a 'My husband's uglier than yours' contest. It was crazy.

Some days, my mother would insist that we took my brother off with us for the day so that they could have a break. He cramped our style though, being so much younger. One day we decided to take him on the rowing boats. Neither me or Tina had ever rowed a boat before (or even sat in one) so we set off with no clue what we were doing. The man pushed us away from the edge and for the next twenty minutes we floundered around in circles without actually getting anywhere. Every time I tried to use my oar I ended up soaking my brother who was sitting at the end of the boat weeping and hanging on like grim death. After a while, the man running the boats took pity on the poor drowned rat in the end of the boat and he dragged us back in. He took our tickets back off us and gave us some to go to the miniature railway instead. He said we would probably be safer in there.

When my mother saw the state of my brother she wasn't best pleased. She'd only let him out of her sight for an hour or two and he had come back soaking wet and traumatised.

"Thank you very much." she snapped "Something else he's bloody scared of now."

He did have a lot of phobias.

On the second to last day me and Tina had a falling out. We had gone to the disco as usual and when I turned round she wasn't there. I went looking for her and caught sight of her disappearing round the corner with the lad who worked in the fish and chip restaurant. I was fuming, she'd just abandoned me. I ran to the corner, shouting for her to come back but she ignored me and carried on walking, arm in arm with him.

I went back inside and joined everyone else, keeping an eye out for her but by the time the disco finished she still wasn't back. Everyone started walking back to their own chalets and I had no choice but to do the same. I walked slowly, hoping she'd find me before I got back, how was I going to explain that I was on my own. I arrived back at the chalet without her and went inside, straight away my parents wanted to know where she was. I tried to fob them off, saying she had forgotten her jacket and she was just behind me but they looked concerned. I knew my dad wouldn't want to attract any attention by reporting her missing.

Just as I was thinking I would have to tell them that she was off somewhere with the fish and chip lad, she came walking in. I shot her an evil look but she just smiled sweetly at my parents and said goodnight. I followed her into our room and we had a blazing argument, conducted in whispers and sign language so that my parents wouldn't hear.

I was accusing her of acting like a slut, going off god knows where to do god knows what with the first lad that looked at her without so much as a backward glance to tell me where she was going. She was equally as furious that I would dare to think she would do anything like that. She said they had spent the time sitting on a bench sharing a bag of chips and talking. What did I think she was and how dare I say things like that about her?

I must say she put a good case. It would have been more convincing though had she not started flinging her clothes around as she got ready for bed. As she threw her top and jacket across the room, half the beach flew out of them, there was sand everywhere. That was the end of the argument, we fell about laughing and had to find a brush to sweep everything up before my mother saw it the next morning.

The next day we had to pack our bags to go home. We went to the cafe early to say goodbye to our new friends, it was quite emotional, with a few of the girls (and the odd boy) crying. Back at the chalet we gathered our bags and waited for the little train to pick us back up and take us to the coach park. It was time to go back to reality and school the next week.

There are a few songs that remind me of that time every time I hear them. 'Young Hearts Run Free' by Candi Statton or 'Heaven Must Be Missing An Angel' by Tevares. Any time I hear them I am instantly transported back to that long, hot summer of 1976. Memories of Butlins, half drowning my brother and watching my dad pouring dirty bath water all over his garden.

Happy days.

CHAPTER EIGHTEEN

It's My Party, I'll Cry If I Want To

It was December again and almost my sixteenth birthday. Unbelievably my parents were allowing me to have a birthday party at my house. Even more unbelievably, they had agreed to go out for the night to leave us to it. Their only rule was that my brother was to be in bed and undisturbed while the party was going on and the music was not to be too loud.

I invited about twenty of my friends, girls and boys and the party was all set for the Friday night. When I got home from school on the Friday afternoon I couldn't believe my eyes, my mother had been baking in preparation for the party. Oh no, not my mother's baking, she would end up making everyone ill. I told her I didn't need anything baked, just a few crisps, peanuts and cocktail sausages on sticks would do.

She wasn't having any of it, she said she had gone to all that trouble and we would bloody well eat it all. She said everyone would be expecting food but I didn't think they'd be expecting food like this. She had baked dozens of scones, jam tarts and a massive gooey chocolate cake. Next to that lot was about three hundred meat paste sandwiches. It looked like an old ladies tea party, not a teenage rave up.

I couldn't argue with her so I let her get on with arranging everything on the dining room table and went off to get ready. My dad had recently started brewing his own beer and said we could have one of

his barrels to drink as long as we took it steady.
Looking back, it was a recipe for disaster.

Around seven o clock everyone started to arrive.
There were about the same number of boys as girls.
We were all just friends, we'd known each other all
through school so there were no romances or anything.
My brother was put to bed and I was given strict
instructions to keep an eye on him and not let anyone
in his room. My mother had recently acquired another
dog, a cross Yorkshire terrier, really small and this was
to be shut up in my brother's room to keep it out of
harm's way.

About half past seven my parents finally left the
house and the party got under way. Straight away
everyone got stuck in to my dad's home brew, it was
horrible but it was strong. They all had a good laugh
about the 'party food' but after a few drinks some of
the boys started eating bits of it.

The music got turned up really loud, even though I
kept protesting, in the end I gave up trying to turn it
down and tried to enjoy myself. It wasn't easy,
everyone was getting really drunk, really quickly.
People were all over the house and I kept trying to
drag them downstairs away from my brother's room.
Some of the lads were in my mother's bedroom
making fun of her nightie while the rest of them
started having a contest to see who could make a scone
stick to the living room wall the longest. It was a
nightmare.

An hour later and it was chaos. People were being
sick in my dad's flower beds outside, someone had
turned the lights out and everyone was dancing in the
dark knocking things all over the place. Drinks were

being spilled all over the carpets and someone had found the dog and let it out of my brother's room. It was running all over the place, scoffing all the sandwiches while some of the girls were screaming that it looked like a rat. Meanwhile my brother was sitting up in bed with his blankets over his head, terrified of all these people in his room trying to offer him a beer. What the hell had I been thinking, asking for a party?

Everyone was having a great time, except me. I was running round like a lunatic trying to clean things up, scrape chocolate cake off the walls and calm down my traumatised brother who was hyperventilating by now.

It was just gone nine o clock and my parents weren't due back until eleven, how was I supposed to keep control until then. At about ten o clock my friend's ex-boyfriend turned up on the doorstep demanding to talk to her and someone let him in. She ended up having a screaming match with him in the hallway, I left them to it. About ten minutes later someone told me that they had finished arguing and they were making up very passionately in the hallway. I went in to try and stop them. That didn't go down well so I shoved them into the downstairs toilet and prayed that they would finish 'making up' before my mother came back and wanted to hang her coat up in there. I was frantic by now.

Thankfully, by about quarter to eleven everyone was on the verge of passing out so I could turn the music down and try to straighten up a bit. I didn't think my mother would see anything too bad when she came in. Surely, she would be expecting a bit of a mess. The couple in the toilet had gone home so that was a weight off my mind and I had threatened my brother with everything I could think of to keep him quiet about what had been going on. The dog had been rounded up and put back in with him so things were a lot quieter now.

At eleven o clock the door opened and in walked my parents. I was quaking in my boots waiting for the hysteria to start. My mother took one look at all the half comatose bodies slumped around the living room and started telling everyone how boring they were.

"Call this a party?" she laughed, then to my horror she turned the music back up and started dancing.

Meanwhile my dad, who had been upstairs to check on my brother, shouted down that someone was in the bath. Oh my god, now what?

It turned out to be Vicky, she was sitting in the empty bath, legs thrown over the side, swigging from a bottle of sparkling wine that she had brought with her. My mother came in and I waited for the shrieking to begin. To my amazement, she burst out laughing and tried to pick Vicky up and drag her out of the bath. Who was this person? I came to the conclusion that my mother must be as drunk as everyone else.

We rounded everyone up and sent them on their way. Vicky sobered up enough to walk home with some of the others and my mother rang her mother to say she was on her way home. Some of the boys had a football match in the morning at school and as the school was nearby and they lived quite far away it had been agreed earlier that they could all bed down in our living room. I was really starting to regret agreeing to this arrangement now. I just wanted all these people out of my house, at that moment I wouldn't have cared if I never saw any of them ever again.

My mother gave all the boys a lecture about being quiet and staying downstairs and then me and my parents went off to bed. For the next hour I could hear them all giggling and talking downstairs. Eventually I got up, put my dressing gown on and went down to give them all a bollocking. I had been through enough for one night and I needed my rest. I crept down quietly so my dad didn't hear me and have a heart attack. Opening the living room door, I told them all to shut up and go to sleep or I would throw them all out even if it was one o clock in the morning. This was met by cries of;

"She's in her nightie, grab her."

Oh, my god, who were these people? Still half drunk they all started dragging me by my dressing gown into the room, laughing hysterically. I was more worried about waking my parents up then being assaulted by this lot. I landed a few punches and slaps and then they realised I wasn't playing. They all said sorry and that they were only messing around and promised to go to sleep. I crept back to my own bed and cursed the day again that I had ever mentioned a birthday party. I felt like I'd aged ten years in the last few hours, I felt more middle aged than I did sixteen. I had seen my mother drunkenly dancing to Gary Glitter while my friends lay around her comatose, I had spent the night cleaning up sick and pulling food from my mother's favourite painting. Now here I was having to fight off a load of lads who had never given me a second glance but now seemed to find me irresistible in my flowered quilted dressing gown.

On top of all that I still had to make sure that my brother kept his mouth firmly shut. This had been one of the worst nights of my life and I just wanted it to be over.

The next morning saw half a dozen, shame faced, hung over, lads who couldn't seem to make eye contact with me. They muttered thank you to my mother for letting them stay the night, clapped me on the back, wished me happy birthday and scarpered as fast as they could. I think they would have escaped before we got up if they could but my dad had locked them all in.

I was never so glad to see the back of anyone. My mother asked if I'd enjoyed my party and I had to force a big smile and say it was great. I vowed there and then that as long as I lived I would never throw another party in my own house.

My brother kept his word and kept his mouth shut, he never dropped me in it. I was greatly relieved and I'm sure the nightmares he had for the next few months were nothing to do with me.

CHAPTER NINETEEN

I'm Feeling Blue

1977 had rolled around and finally I was in my last year at school, I couldn't wait to get away. For some reason that year the kids that were good at English had been allowed to take their 'O' level exam early and I was one of them. Instead of taking it in the summer with all the other exams we were taking it in February.

I had already decided I wasn't sticking around to take exams. As I was already sixteen I could leave at Easter, three months before the official end of term. I was already looking for a job. My parents didn't encourage me to take my exams as most parents would. My mother said the sooner I got a job the better, she could use the extra board money. Bless her she always wanted the best for me.

A few days before the exam I decided what my hair needed was some blonde highlights. Now I was sixteen my parents considered me old enough to look as stupid as I wanted, after all they had made me look stupid for the first twelve, now it was up to me. I asked Janice to do it for me and she agreed. On the Sunday I went round to Aunty Dolly's so she could transform me into a blonde bombshell. She shoved a rubber cap down onto my head and began attacking me with a crochet hook, pulling bits of hair through the holes in the cap. She was very rough, I was hoping she didn't treat the clients at her work as roughly as this or she would never make much in tips.

When she was finished pulling half my hair through the rubber cap she mixed up a load of bleach and plastered it all over my head. It smelt really bad and my eyes were watering, I was made to stay in the kitchen so that I didn't drip on the carpets. It was only a small kitchen and my Aunty Dolly had to keep climbing over me to get in the cupboards. Malcom kept walking by and sniggering at the sight of me. Every ten minutes Janice would wipe a bit of the bleach off with a bit of cotton wool, then she would say it wasn't ready yet and slap a bit more on. It took forever, I was bored to tears and the cap was giving me a headache.

After what seemed like hours Janice did a final inspection and said it was ready. We went up to the bathroom and she washed all the bleach off. When she pulled the cap off I began to think half my hair was going with it but it stayed attached to my head and the relief was great as the pressure of the cap was lifted off. She shampooed and conditioned it and then we went back downstairs so she could blow dry it. At this stage I still hadn't seen it as she wanted to show me the big transformation when it was all finished.

She messed around with it for a while, using different brushes while she dried it, eventually it was finished. She dragged me over to the mirror to show me her handywork. I didn't know what to say. Instead of the subtle blonde highlights that I had wanted, more than half of my hair was so blonde that it was white. I had been hoping for a sunkissed look, what I was looking at was an old aged pensioner. I was horrified. Janice saw my face and said it wasn't her fault, she had done exactly as I asked. I think somewhere down the line we had got our wires crossed.

I walked home feeling sick. I had to go to school in the morning and there was nowhere open on a Sunday where I could buy any hair dye to cover it all up. My parents did a double take when I walked through the door. My dad just shook his head while my mother said it made me look older. She was right, about sixty years older. I would have to sort it out after school tomorrow, the day after that I was sitting my exam and I couldn't concentrate if I was worrying about my hair. Before that I would have to face everyone at school and hope they would believe me when I told them it was the latest thing.

They didn't. Everyone laughed themselves silly. All day I had to put up with jokes about walking sticks, wheel chairs and incontinence pants. At dinner time Vicky rushed home and came back with a box of hair dye that she'd bought but never used, it was Raven Black. My normal hair colour was mid to dark brown but black would do, anything was better than this.

After school, I rushed home, ignoring the shouts from some of the lads in my class,

"Mind how you go, you don't want to break a hip."

As soon as I got in I locked myself in the bathroom with the hair dye. I slapped it on and waited thirty minutes like it said on the box. After ten minutes it already looked a lot darker this was going to work I would be ok. When it was done, I rinsed it all off and looked in the mirror. It was very black, I looked a bit like a vampire but that was better than looking like a pensioner. I wrapped my head in a towel and went off to dry it.

After a few minutes with the hairdryer I realised something was wrong. My normal hair was jet black but the highlights were beginning to show again. This time instead of being white they were pale blue. What the hell had gone wrong now?

Grabbing the box, I read the label (probably should have done that before), the label said Raven Black which I already knew. Next to that in smaller letters it said, 'blue/black'. Oh god, I had blue hair. The more I dried it the more the blue stood out, my mother would have a fit. My dad would have a stroke, this would cause his worst nightmare, people would look at us.

I bit the bullet and went downstairs to show my mother, maybe it wasn't that noticeable. She took one look at me and let out a scream that could probably be heard in the next street.

"What have you done you stupid bugger?" she sympathised. "Your dad will be home soon, he'll have a blue fit."

I wanted to tell her at least he would match my hair but I was too miserable.

I went back upstairs and washed my hair again. Maybe it would fade a bit.

It didn't so I washed it again, and again, and again. It made no difference at all, the only thing that happened was my hands got sore and I used up all the hot water. Finally, my mother stepped in and banned me from washing it again. She said my hair would fall out if I kept washing and drying it. By this time my dad was home, he took one look at me and disappeared behind his newspaper but not before telling me this is what happens if you mess around with yourself.

All night I worried about school the next day, I had to go because it was exam day. I wondered if I could get away with wearing a hat all day but that would only attract attention anyway and everyone would want to know what was under it. In the end, there was nothing for it but to face the music (and the howls of laughter).

I walked into class the next day and endured all the wise cracks and jokes. Vicky was dead sorry that she hadn't read the box properly she said but I swear when she turned away she was sniggering as well. When it was time to go into the hall for the exam I held my blue head high and went to take it.

All the way through the exam I could see people sneaking peeks at the old lady with the blue rinse. Punk rock hadn't really reached our town yet so the only people we ever saw with blue or purple hair were old ladies who had gone a bit bonkers. I sat there trying to pretend that I was ahead of my time and that soon everyone would want blue hair. I don't think I was very convincing.

Finally, the exam was over and I could go home. I sometimes wonder if some of the kids would have got a better grade if it wasn't for me sitting in the front row distracting everyone with my cutting edge 'do'.

Arriving home I begged my mother for a pound to go and buy a brown dye to cover all the blue. She refused, she said it would teach me a lesson not to mess about with my hair if I had to live with it a bit longer. I was horrified but that wasn't the end of it. She also said I wasn't allowed to wash it again for at least a week, she said I had stripped all the oils out of it and it was likely to fall out. I would have to walk around for a week with blue hair. I knew when my dad came home he would take my side, he wouldn't want a blue haired daughter for any longer than he had to, he would save me.

He didn't. He said it was up to my mother and he wasn't going to go against her. I was stuffed, to top it all I had to be followed every time I went to the bathroom. My mother said she didn't trust me not to wash my hair sneakily so every time I needed a wee someone would wait outside the door, it was crazy.

I thought I would be ok when they went for their usual night out, I could wash it then but they were already ahead of me. They roped in Joan next door to help. Whenever we ran water in our house Joan could hear our pipes in her house. They told her if she heard water running she had permission to come in and stop me washing my hair. I was under hair wash arrest.

This carried on for five days before my mother took pity on me. I don't know if it was the sight of me floating around the house in a headscarf looking like a Russian peasant or my dad's fear of the neighbours seeing me. I didn't care so long as this was going to be over. My mother gave me a pound and told me to go to the chemist and buy a brown dye.

An hour later I was more or less back to normal. It was a bit darker than usual but anything was better than being blue. My parents said they hoped I had learnt my lesson and I assured them that I had, nothing would make me dye my hair ever again.

I kept my word for at least six months. Throughout the years my hair has been many shades and colours but it has never been blue again. Never say never though, when I get to be seventy odd I may get a yen for a blue rinse like all the other old ladies. By then I won't care as I will be growing old disgracefully and at least my dad won't be around to see it.

CHAPTER TWENTY

Working Girl

I was down to my last two weeks at school. It was nearly over and I couldn't wait to get away and start working for a living. The week before I had been for an interview for a shop assistant's job, working in a new bakery shop that was opening. They would be selling bread, cakes, pastries and cold meats. I had heard a few days ago that I had got the job and I would be earning £14 per week. That was a small fortune to me, I had never had that much money to myself. My mother was happy too as she had already earmarked £5 of it every week for her pocket.

I had to spend the first two weeks being trained at the company's big shop in the town centre before being moved to the new shop on opening day. I had already got my uniform, a really fetching white nylon overall, dead glamorous. All I had to do now was get through the last two weeks of school and I could get started on life as a grown-up person.

Those last two weeks dragged on and on, it felt like two months. All of my friends were staying on until the summer to take their exams. I didn't care about exams, I was rubbish at maths, art and everything else so I knew I wouldn't get good grades anyway. Besides that, I already had the English 'O' level that I had passed during my blue hair period, despite all the stress and embarrassment, I had managed to get a B plus. I always thought that if my hair hadn't been blue I would have got an A.

At last the day came when I could escape forever. The last ten years of homicidal teachers and humiliating clothes and haircuts would be nothing more than a memory now. I was free.

When it came time to walk out of the gates for the last time it was bit of an anti-climax really. It was just like any other day, there was no fuss, no fireworks or people crying, afraid they would never see me again. Everyone just said, "See you later" and that was it. Mind you, they would see me later, it was the under-eighteen's disco that night. It felt really strange when I arrived home, knowing I would never leave the house to go to school again.

I soon got over it and began to prepare for the world of work. My dad gave me lots of advice about keeping my head down, not making a fuss and getting on with the job. That was his motto for life really, get through the day without being noticed. As I would be serving customers dressed in a bright white nylon overall, I didn't think I would be able to go un noticed, but I told him I would do my best.

When my first day came around I set off to catch the bus into town. I was really nervous, it felt strange to be on a bus so early in the morning among all the other people setting off to work. When I got there I was shown to the meat and savoury counter. I was going to be serving sausage rolls, pork pies and weighing out cold meats. After I had got the hang of that they would put me onto the bread and pastry counter. It was a really busy shop and after serving a few people I got into the swing of things. If there was anything I wasn't sure of I could ask one of the other girls. The worst part was the adding up, there was no till to do it for you, if you couldn't do it in your head you had to add it all up on a piece of paper. Being so rubbish at maths I was dreading this but it was just simple adding up and after a while you got used to all the prices anyway.

I was introduced to the other girl who would be working at the new shop with me. Her name was Cheryl and she had just left school like me. We had a lot in common and during our lunch break we discovered that we had both been at the same primary school together. We both remembered the other kids and the teachers but we didn't remember each other. We had grown up just a few streets apart and played on the same playground.

The first two weeks in training flew by. Because the shop was right in the middle of town it was always really busy, there was no time to get bored. Me and Cheryl had both got the hang of things now and it felt like we had been doing the job for ages. Soon it was our last day, we said goodbye on the Saturday teatime and arranged to meet at the new shop on the Monday. Then I went home with my £14 wages burning a hole in my pocket. That was the only thing that really bothered me, I had to work Saturdays now. No more going in town with my friends shopping and eating chips for dinner any more, just when I finally had money to spend as well. I only had Mondays off and that would be no fun as my friends would all still be in school. Oh well, if I wasn't spending it I would be able to save up a bit. As long as I hid it from my mother.

The first morning at the new shop we met the manager, Mr Sweeny. It was hate at first sight. He was one of the most horrible people I ever had the misfortune to meet, even now it's hard to think of anyone else who was so awful. He was tall, thin, pale and ginger with a face that looked like he was chewing a lemon. Unfortunately, he had a personality to match. He always looked at us as if we were a bad smell under his nose and he was rude and vindictive. Later on, we would find out that he was also fond of pushing and shoving us young ones about, it was school all over again.

We had got used to the nice atmosphere in the other shop and we weren't prepared for this one. As soon as Mr Sweeny stepped out of the back and into the shop it was like a big black cloud had settled over us.

Everybody hated him, staff and customers alike. We soon found our way around the new shop though and started to settle in. Me and Cheryl were still working on the meat and savoury counter. The cakes, buns and bread were sold from the counter opposite ours.

The first morning went by really quickly, it was nonstop, because it was a new shop everyone had come out to have a look. Me and Cheryl grabbed a quick sandwich for our lunch break and then got back to work. Because it was so busy Mr Sweeny was helping to serve the customers. He did everything at top speed, charging around the shop from counter to counter shouting for the next customer. He practically threw the goods at the poor people in the queue, he was like a demented ferret weaving in and out of us all and scolding us for getting in his way.

My first afternoon there, a little man came in and stood at my counter. I asked if I could help him and he nodded. He then tried to ask me for what he wanted and I discovered he had the worst stutter I had ever heard. To make matters worse he wanted six savoury sausage rolls. Now that's hard to say at the best of times but when you've got a terrible stutter it must be hell. He gave it a go anyway and began to speak,

"Sss…. Sss…. sss …iiii … xxx… sss…"

Then nothing else would come out. I could see what he was looking at so to help the poor bugger out I asked him if he meant the sausage rolls. He smiled and nodded gratefully so I started to put them in a bag. Immediately, Mr Sweeny was at my elbow.

"Don't patronise the man" he hissed "Let him finish his sentence."

The poor little man looked horrified, so did I for that matter but he had to start all over again, stuttering and stuttering trying to ask for his six, savoury sausage rolls.

It was excruciating. He was turning purple with the effort of trying to get his words out but Mr Sweeny just stood there staring at him the whole time. It took him about ten minutes to get the words out and by that time I felt like asking him if he wouldn't rather have plain ones.

Eventually he got through it and I put his sausage rolls in a bag for him, I felt awful when he left but then Mr Sweeny started on me.

"Don't you ever do that again." he said "People like that don't like it when you help them, you stand there and let him get it out even if it takes all day."
I didn't think the poor man would agree with him but I doubted I'd ever see him again anyway, nobody would come back to be put through all that again.

I was wrong. Two days later he was back, wanting the same thing. I knew he was waiting for me to say I knew what he wanted and just put his sausage rolls in a bag but I could see Mr Sweeny watching me, waiting to see if I would disobey him and help the man. Again it took him ages to get the words out, I wanted the ground to open up and swallow the pair of us. Eventually, we got there and he went on his way again. After that he came in every other day. If Mr Sweeny wasn't around I would just get him his sausage rolls as soon as I saw him and he was always really grateful. If Mr Sweeny was there though, we would have to go through the whole performance again. I'm sure he got some perverse pleasure from watching the poor man suffer.

One day a few weeks later Mr Sweeny got his come uppance. It was a busy Saturday morning and he was charging around like a maniac as usual. We sold some really odd stuff on the meat counter and one of the weirdest things was Chitterlings. These were the small intestines of a pig and they looked revolting, all slimy and horrible. I don't know what people did with them but we sold a lot. What none of us realised on this morning was that someone had dropped a small piece on the floor (I swear it wasn't me). Mr Sweeny was running from one counter to the other like a maniac when his heel hit the wet, slimy chitterling and he went flying, skidding across the floor, greasy ginger hair flying out behind him. He sailed the full length of our counter before crashing into the bacon slicer and disappearing from sight into the back.

The whole shop erupted with laughter. Me and Cheryl were holding each other up, crying with laughter even though we knew we would pay for it later. Barbara, who worked on the cake counter, had slipped to the floor and was rolling around in hysterics and all the customers were helpless with laughter. When Mr Sweeny appeared again, his face all red and furious, all the customers gave him a big round of applause. He was beside himself with rage.

"You and you" he screamed pointing at me and Cheryl. "In the back, NOW."

We followed him, knees quaking while all the customers shouted at him to leave us alone. I was willing them to stop, they would only make him madder.

When we got into the back he rounded on us.

"Who did it?" He hissed, his nose about an inch from ours.

"Was it you?" (poke in the chest for Cheryl).

"Or you?" (poke in the chest for me).

We both denied all knowledge, we weren't the only ones working on the meat counter that day. For all we knew he had dropped it himself while he was charging around like a mad thing.

He ranted and raved for another ten minutes before he told us to get out of his sight and get back to work. Which we did, gladly.

Things carried on like that for the next few weeks. We hated going to work, the staff and customers were all really nice, it was just Mr Sweeny that spoiled it. Once a week he had a day off and the mood in the shop would lift, it was like the sun coming out. We would have one glorious day, then he would come back and the mood would turn black again. If he was in a bad mood with us for something, the pushing and poking would continue. I told my mother about it but she just told me,

"Don't do anything to make him mad then."

In the shop, we sold pig fries for 10p, these consisted of a mixture of pig's liver, kidneys, heart and brains all slapped onto a piece of greaseproof paper. It was a revolting mix but even worse was I had to make them up. It was supposed to be done on a rota but it was always my turn, I had to stand in the back with a giant container of liver swimming in blood. I had to chop the liver into pieces, weigh it out and then add kidneys, heart and brain, all cut up and weighed. It was a horrible job and the smell was horrendous. For the first time I was starting to miss school.

Me and Cheryl started hanging around together outside work. We went out some nights and she came to my house a few times. After a while she decided it would be a good idea to set me up with her brother, he was two years older than us and had a reputation as a 'bad lad'. Cheryl adored him and decided that all he needed to settle him down was a good woman - me. I told her I didn't want a boyfriend, I was going to be young free and single and play the field. She took no notice and set us up anyway.

She showed me a picture that she carried around in her bag and said she'd shown him a picture of me and he was all for it. In the end, I went along with it to shut her up and she brought him, along with her boyfriend to my house. I didn't recognise him from the photo and thought she must have brought me a replacement. He says as soon as I opened the door he made his mind up to marry me. He swears I was wearing a Bay City Rollers top but it was a black top that just happened to have a bit of tartan on the collar. My Bay City Rollers phase was way behind me by then. He had also been at my primary school but I didn't remember him either.

I thought he was ok but it wasn't love at first sight on my part. I said goodnight to them all at the end of the night and that was that. The next day at work Cheryl was dying to know what I thought, didn't we make a perfect couple, blah, blah. I told her he was nice enough but I didn't know if I wanted to see him again. It turned out I didn't have a choice, when lunch time came around, there he was, waiting outside the shop for me. I was a bit surprised but Cheryl was over the moon.

From that day on he stalked me everywhere I went. He would take two buses and roll up at my house just as I was settling down to watch Coronation Street. He worked on a building site a mile or so from our shop and he would drive his dumper truck all the way there to meet me at lunch time, there was no escaping him. He brought my mother chocolates and was nice to my little brother so eventually my parents started to warm to him. I was in a relationship and I wasn't even sure how it had happened.

When one day he didn't turn up at work and I didn't hear from him for two days I realised I didn't like it. Where was he, what was he doing, was I dumped? I discovered I actually quite missed him. I started quizzing Cheryl, she lived in the same house, she must know what was going on, what was he up to? She said she didn't know, he was acting just the same as usual.

The next day he showed up as normal. He had been trying the 'absence makes the heart grow fonder' thing he said. I smacked him round the head, told him he was lucky it wasn't 'out of sight, out of mind' and nearly thirty six years later he's still here.

Even today, all these years later he is still trying to convince me that I was the little girl with glasses who he showed his willy to under the desk back in primary school. I have been telling him for the same amount of years that it wasn't me. For one thing he is two years older than me so we wouldn't even have been in the same class, and I think if anyone had shown me a willy when I was that young I would have been so traumatised I would have remembered.

Back at the shop things were still horrible. One morning one of the older women who worked there told us she'd heard a rumour that Mr Sweeny was trying to find jobs for some relatives of his. She told us to watch out or he would find some excuse to get rid of us and replace us with them. The following Saturday I gave him his chance.

It was really busy and as one of the girls who worked on the bread and cake counter was off sick, I was promoted for the day and went to fill in for her. The morning went fine, it was a nice change to be away from the pig's innards and the pork pies although I wouldn't have cared if I never saw a cream bun again. After lunch, it got even busier, the queue was really long and we were rushed off our feet. One lady asked for some sort of cake that wasn't on display on the counter, she said there was one in the window so I went to get it for her. I should have known better.

The cake was on the bottom shelf at the front of the window so I crouched down and leaned forward until I reached it. So far so good. Unfortunately, as I went to stand back up again I caught one of the shelves with my shoulder and sent it, and all its cream filled contents flying. That shelf hit another shelf which in turn hit another and before I knew what was happening the entire window full of cream cakes were flying everywhere. It was like an explosion in a cream factory. Everyone in the shop let out one collective "Ooops" which brought Mr Sweeny running out from the back.

I crouched down under the counter, too terrified to stand back up and face him. "Who did this?" he screeched,

"Who is responsible for this?"

I figured I couldn't stay down there all day so I stood up to face him, I couldn't really deny it anyway, seeing as I was covered in jam and cream.

"In the back, NOW" he screamed.

I was getting used to hearing this now. I went slinking off behind him to face my punishment, I figured that was me gone, I never liked this job anyway.

He didn't sack me, he screamed and bawled for a bit and then told me all the damage would be coming out of my wages, then he told me to clean myself up and get back to work. I did as I was told but I thought my days there were probably numbered, it was just a case of waiting for the hammer to fall.

I didn't have to wait long. On the Monday morning before we even started work Mr Sweeny called me over and told me my services were no longer needed, as he put it,

"Things aren't working out."

It was a relief really, I couldn't wait to get out of there, I was more annoyed that he hadn't sacked me on the Saturday. He'd made me come all the way back here for nothing, I'd wasted my bus fares.

As I left I saw Cheryl's shocked face, I shouted that I'd phone her later and then I was gone. A week later she would be following me out the door and a week after that Mr Sweeny's relatives had both our jobs.

My mother was mortified that I had been sacked. No one in our family had ever been sacked. How would she ever hold her head up around the neighbours now? Never mind that I had been getting physically assaulted at work, she didn't care about that.

Ever since I had started work she had been getting some of my wages changed into coins for my bus fares, she did this every week at the social club my parents went to. To keep up appearances she kept on doing this for weeks even when I wasn't going anywhere. I was banned from telling anyone that I had been sacked.

This went on for a few weeks until, much to her relief I got another job. This time I was working in a clothes shop, my boss was a Pakistani man. He was very nice but he had some strange ideas. On my third day there the girl that had been working with me didn't show up. When I asked him where she was he said he had sacked her for being fat. He said fat people didn't work properly, they were too lazy. Even back then this was quite shocking.

A few weeks after that, he decided I wouldn't be having lunch hours any more. He said if he stopped me eating lunch it would ensure that I didn't get fat like the other girl. I figured my mother would soon be feeling ashamed again. I didn't think much to this working lark, I had been pushed and poked in my first job and starved in my second.

Finally, I found another job, working in a little supermarket not far from home. This was a nice job and I stayed there until I left to have my daughter some years later. I never really had any mishaps in this job, I think the worst thing I ever did was make a mistake with the ordering and end up with 240 jars of piccalilli instead of 24. In a big place it wouldn't have mattered but there we only sold about half a dozen jars a year. The warehouse lad helped me hide them all over the place in the stock room, we hid trays and trays of them on all the high shelves behind other things. By the time I left we had only sold three trays of them. Sometimes I think some of them must still be up there.

Soon after starting that job I got the second proposal of my life, almost as romantic as my first one when I was eight. By this time my future husband was working shifts in a factory. He would work until ten o clock at night, then cycle all the way to my house (about seven miles) to see me for an hour before cycling home again. One night he arrived exhausted and told me his legs couldn't take all this cycling, we would have to get married. What girl wouldn't want to hear that?

When I told my parents the next morning, they were a bit shocked to say the least, I was only seventeen. My dad thought the worst but couldn't actually ask me himself if I was pregnant, he got my mother to ask me. I wasn't but I don't think she was that bothered about that anyway, all she cared about was losing my board money. I figured she'd better get my brother's name down for a paper round.

So there I was at the ripe old age of seventeen and a half, steady job, engaged to be married, and in charge of my own clothes and haircuts. I would have liked to go back and tell the seven year old me that there was light at the end of that long dark tunnel filled with horrible clothes, excruciating hairstyles and embarrassing glasses.

I was about to escape forever and become a proper grown up.

What would fate have in store for me now?

THE END
(For now)

29397410R00090

Printed in Great Britain
by Amazon